W9-CCQ-781

Have a Good Laugh:
Jokes for the Jewish Soul

Have a Good Laugh:
Jokes for the Jewish Soul

Ron Isaacs

Illustrations by
Franklin Feldman

KTAV Publishing House, Inc.

Copyright©2009 Ronald H. Isaacs

Library of Congress Cataloging-in-Publication Data

Isaacs, Ronald H.
  Have a good laugh : jokes for the Jewish soul / Ron Isaacs ;
illustrations by Franklin Feldman.
      p. cm.
  ISBN 978-1-60280-130-1
  1. Jewish wit and humor. I. Title.

PN6231.J5I83 2009
818'.5402--dc22

2009027027

Published by
KTAV Publishing House, Inc.
930 Newark Avenue
Jersey City, NJ 07306
Email: bernie@ktav.com
www.ktav.com
(201) 963-9524
Fax (201) 963-0102

Table of Contents

Table of Contents

Table of Contents

Table of Contents

Table of Contents

Acknowledgments

I wish to thank a few people for helping bring this book to fruition. First, to Bernie Scharfstein, a good friend and creative thinker, whose idea it was to create this Joke book in the first place. To my colleague Rabbi Stanley Schachter for granting me permission to use some of the jokes appearing his outstanding volume *Laugh for God's Sake: Where Jewish Humor and Jewish Ethics Meet (Ktav)*. My appreciation goes out to Deanna Alpher, Stanley Stein, Alvin Rosenthal and the Internet for providing me with additional jokes for this book. And finally, much appreciation to Franklin Feldman for his outstanding illustrations.

Introduction

The Jewish people have a long tradition of humor, dating back to the Jewish Bible and the Talmud. Its topics are universal: business, food, family, religion, sickness, and survival. The *Book of Esther*, read on the festival of Purim, likely one of the most well known books among modern Jews, is replete with biblical humor. Very often synagogue members perform humorous skits (*spiels*) during the Megillah reading and on the day of Purim itself, often using somewhat irreverent humor and jokes, all intended to add to the festival's frivolity. The talmudic rabbis also had a keen sense of humor, as is evident from their numerous witty sayings in the talmudic and midrashic literature. The fourth-century Babylonian rabbi known as Rabbah delivered his lectures in a serious frame of mind but would always preface them with a joke or witticism, believing that by making his students smile he would help them to appreciate better the complicated subjects he intended to teach them. Even God is said to have a sense of humor, as the Psalmist writes: "The One who sits in heaven shall laugh." Since we are to emulate God in all of God's attributes, why not laugh along with the Holy Blessed One?

A talmudic legend (*Ta'anit* 22a) tells of Elijah pointing out to a rabbi two men in the marketplace who were assured of a place in the World to Come. When the rabbi asked them the nature of their occupation, they said that they were comedians who brought cheer into the lives of sufferers by amusing them with their witticisms. In some talmudic arguments humor is even introduced in order to support a case.

Even the great Sigmund Freud, an avowed atheist, chose to write a book on humor, which he called *Jokes and Their Relation to the Unconscious*. The book contains a great deal of information on Jewish humor, as Freud was especially impressed about how Jews were free to make light and fun of their shortcomings, using humor as an escape hatch to express repressed urges through jokes. In his book *Jewish Literacy*, Joseph Telushkin cites one of Freud's favorite jokes. The tale is told of a Jewish beggar who "approached a wealthy baron with a request for some assistance for his journey to [the resort of] Ostend. The doctors, he said, had recommended sea-bathing to restore his health. 'Very well,' said the rich man, 'I'll give you something towards it. But must you go precisely to Ostend, which is the most expensive of all sea-bathing resorts?' 'Herr Baron,' was the reproachful reply, 'I consider nothing too expensive for my health'" (Joseph Telushkin, *Jewish Literacy*. New York: William Morrow, p. 252).

One of the most recent and novel approaches to Jewish humor is that of Rabbi Stanley J. Schachter, whose book *Laugh for God's Sake* studies the connection between Jewish humor and its connection to Jewish ethics. His thoughtful analysis uncovers Jewish humor as an active partner of Judaism's Talmud Torah, timeless teachings, couched in laughter, and intended to remind Jews of their ethical obligations in life.

Introduction

Whether ancient or modern, Jewish humor largely concerns and continues to concern itself with topics of everyday life. It continues to occupy a special place in American popular culture. *Have a Good Laugh: Jokes for the Jewish Soul* is not meant to study Jewish humor, but rather to present a collection of Jewish jokes that are meant to bring a smile to your face and tickle your fancy. If you are a professional or even an amateur speaker, you can use this book as a source of humorous stories with which to beguile your audiences at lectures or parties. Because Judaism and rabbinic tradition have always placed such a high value on the proper use of words, the two hundred and fifty jokes in this book have been carefully selected. So don't expect to find crude or offensive jokes in this volume. Additionally, the jokes appear topically for easy access, and include the following chapters: Rabbis, Theology and God, Family, Bible, Israel, Humor from Chelm, and a section that includes a potpourri of Jewish humor on a variety of topics.

May the humor in this volume give you much delight and make you smile. Have fun, enjoy, give a chuckle—and let the laughter begin!

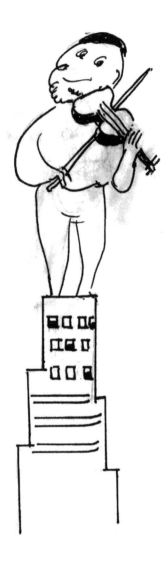

Chapter One
Israel

The Land of Israel is the birthplace of the Jewish people. Here the spiritual, political, and religious identity of the people was shaped. Ancient Israel also created the cultural values of national and universal significance that gave rise to the Bible. Few countries have as many special attractions per square mile as Israel. When one adds the depth of feeling for the country shared by Jews around the world, its unique appeal becomes more obvious. This chapter will present some jokes about Israel, the land, and its people.

☺ ☺ ☺ ☺ ☺ ☺ ☺ ☺

The Unexpected Delivery
Moshe, the owner of a small Kosher New York deli, was being questioned by an IRS agent about his tax return. He had reported a net profit of $80,000 for the year.

'Why don't people leave me alone?' the deli owner said. 'I work like a dog, everyone in my family helps out, the place is only closed for Jewish Holidays and Shabbat. And you want to know how I made $80,000?'

'It's not your income that bothers us,' the agent said. 'It's these travel deductions. You listed ten trips to Israel for you and your wife.'

'Oh, that?' the owner said smiling. 'Well... We also deliver.'

☺ ☺ ☺ ☺ ☺ ☺ ☺ ☺

The Taxi

An American tourist was riding in a taxi in Israel. As the taxi approached a red light, the tourist was shocked to see the driver drive straight through without even slowing down. Surprised as he was, he didn't say anything, feeling himself a guest and not wanting to make waves.

The trip continued without event until the next intersection. This time the light was green, and, to the American's dismay, the cab driver brought the vehicle to a grinding halt.

Unable to contain his astonishment, he turns to the driver. "Listen," he says, "when you went through the red light, I didn't say anything. But why on earth are you stopping at a green light?"

The Israeli driver looks at the American as if he is deranged. "Are you crazy?" he shouts. "The other guy has a red light. Do you want to get us killed?"

☺ ☺ ☺ ☺ ☺ ☺ ☺ ☺

The Three Hunters

Three hunters are out on safari—an American, a Brit, and an Israeli. They are captured by cannibals who start getting the cooking pots ready. The cannibal chief tells the hunters that they can have one last wish,

"What's your request?" he asks the American.

"I'd like steak," he replies.

So the cannibals kill a zebra and serve the American his steak.

"What do you want?" the cannibal asks the Brit.

"I'd like to smoke my pipe," which they let him do.

Then the chief asks the Israeli, "What's your last wish?"

"I want you to kick my rear end."

"Be serious," says the top cannibal.

"C'mon, you promised," says the Israel.

"Oh, all right," says the chief, who delivers the requested kick.

Whereupon the Israeli pulls out a gun, shoots the chief, and a few other cannibals while the rest run away.

The American and the Brit are furious.

"Why didn't you do that in the first place, so we wouldn't have to go through all this?" they demand.

Replies the Israeli, "What? Are you mad? The UN would have condemned me as the aggressor."

☺ ☺ ☺ ☺ ☺ ☺ ☺ ☺

Jerusalem Jaywalking

The jaywalking problem in New York City reminded me of a time when my husband and I were on a visit to Jerusalem. As we waited patiently at a busy intersection for the "walk" signal, a young man sped across the street against the light. An elderly gentleman waiting with us turned and said sadly, "Two thousand years he's waiting for the Messiah, and he can't wait for a light."

☺ ☺ ☺ ☺ ☺ ☺ ☺ ☺

Airplane Announcement
An El Al flight is about to take off. Over the intercom the passengers hear: "Ladies and gentlemen, welcome aboard. Your hostesses are Mrs. Sarah Klein, Mrs. Miriam Stern, and Mrs. Esther Kling. Now let me introduce you to my son the pilot."

☺ ☺ ☺ ☺ ☺ ☺ ☺ ☺

Man and Wife
An Israeli mayor in a small town is walking past a construction site with his wife. One of the construction workers stops and call out to the woman. "What's new Sara?"

"Why, it's nice to see you again, Avi," the woman replies. She turns to introduce her husband to the construction worker, and they speak for several minutes.

After the mayor and his wife continue on, he turns to his wife to ask how she knows him.

"Oh," she said. "We went together in high school. I even thought about marrying him."

The husband began to laugh. "You don't realize how lucky you are. If I hadn't come along today, you would be the wife of a construction worker."

The wife replied without hesitation: "Not really. If I had married him, he'd now be a mayor."

☺ ☺ ☺ ☺ ☺ ☺ ☺ ☺

Airliner Laugh
The captain of a Syrian airliner announces, "This is Syrian Airliner 174. We have an emergency. We have lost an en-

gine and want to land at any airport in the Middle East other than Israel."

No answer.

A short while later, things get worse, "This is Syrian Airliner 174 again. We have lost two engines and ask permission to land at any airport in the Mideast other than Israel."

Again, no answer from anyone.

A little later the pilot in desperation says, "This is Syrian Airliner 174. We are in need of help. We have lost three engines and need permission to land at any airport in the Mideast other than Israel."

Still no answer from anyone.

Finally, the Captain calls "help." This is Syrian Airliner 174, we have only one engine left, and it is rapidly failing. Unless we can land, we are going to crash. We need permission to land at any airport in the Mideast, including Israel."

Shortly thereafter, a voice is heard in the Syrian airline cockpit: "This is Tel Aviv airport calling Syrian Airliner 174. We would like to help."

"God bless you," said the Syrian pilot. "What should we do?"

Responded Tel Aviv airport, "Repeat after me: Yisgadal ve-yisgadash . . ." (first Hebrew words of Jewish Mourner's Prayer).

☺ ☺ ☺ ☺ ☺ ☺ ☺ ☺

The Thousand-Dollar Bet

The local bar in Jerusalem was so sure that its bartender was the strongest man around that they offered a standing one-thousand-dollar bet. The bartender would squeeze a lemon until all the juice ran into a glass, and hand the lemon to a patron. Anyone who could squeeze one more drop of juice out would win the money. People of many professions tried it over time, but nobody was successful.

One day this scrawny Jewish man came into the bar with thick glasses and a polyester suit, and said in a squeaky voice "I'd like to try the bet." After the laughter subsided, the bartender said okay, grabbed a lemon, and squeezed away. Then he handed the wrinkled remains of the rind to the Jewish man.

But the crowd's laughter soon turned to total silence as the man clenched his fist around the lemon and six drops fell into the glass! As the crowd now cheered, the bartender paid the one thousand dollars, and asked the little Jewish man: "What do you do for a living? Are you a lumberjack or a weightlifter?"

The Jewish guy replied: "I work for the Jewish National Fund."

☺ ☺ ☺ ☺ ☺ ☺ ☺ ☺

What's the Time?

An Israeli was telling his neighbor, "I just bought a brand new hearing aid. It cost me four thousand dollars, but it's state of the art. It's "maxeem" (extraordinary).

"Really," asked the neighbor. "What kind is it?"
"Twelve thirty."

☺ ☺ ☺ ☺ ☺ ☺ ☺ ☺

Captured Israelis
Eight Arabs were about to shoot two captured Israelis. One of the Israelis said to the other, "I think I'm going to be asked to be blindfolded."

The other said, "Look, Shmuel, don't make trouble."

☺ ☺ ☺ ☺ ☺ ☺ ☺ ☺

The Pope Visits the Holy Land
A picture of an Israeli newspaper, during the Pope's visit in 1964, showed the Pope with the President of Israel. The caption greatly helped the mystified readers: "The Pope is the one wearing a yarmulke" (skull cap).

☺ ☺ ☺ ☺ ☺ ☺ ☺ ☺

The Shouting Israeli
On the border, on top of a hill, there is an Israeli guard. On the other side is an Arab guard. All day long, the Israeli keeps shouting, "Ten, ten, ten, ten."

This very much annoys the Arab, who finally shouts at him, "Crazy Jew, why do you keep shouting *ten* all day. There's nobody around here. Ten what?"

The Israeli says, "If you really want to know, come here and I will show you. There, now look over the cliff."

He kicks the Arab over the cliff, clears his throat, and starts yelling, "Eleven, eleven, eleven."

☺   ☺   ☺   ☺   ☺   ☺   ☺   ☺

Lenin's Bust

An old Jewish man was finally allowed to leave the Soviet Union to immigrate to Israel. When he was searched at the Moscow airport, the customs official found a bust of Lenin.

Customs: "What is that?"

Old Man: "What is that? Don't say 'What is that?' Say, 'Who is that?' That is Lenin. The genius who thought up this worker's paradise."

The official laughed and let the old man through. The old man arrived at Tel Aviv airport, where an Israeli customs official found the bust of Lenin.

Customs: "What is that?"

Old Man: "What is that? Don't say, 'What is that?' Say, 'Who is that?' That is Lenin. That S.O.B. I will put him on display in my toilet for all the years he prevented an old man from coming home."

The official laughed and let him through. When he arrived at his family's house in Jerusalem his grandson saw him unpack the bust.

Grandson: "Who is that?"

Old Man: "Who is that?! Don't say, 'Who is that?' Say, 'What is that?' That, my child, is eight pounds of gold!"

☺   ☺   ☺   ☺   ☺   ☺   ☺   ☺

Where to Be Buried

A good old American Jew felt that death is close and asked his sons to take him to the Holy Land, to die there and be buried in Jerusalem. The loving sons did as he asked, brought him to Jerusalem, and put him in a hospital, and waited for death to come. However, once in Jerusalem the old man felt better and better and in some weeks was again strong, healthy, and full of life. He called upon his sons and told them: "Take me quickly back to the United States."

The sons were somewhat disappointed and asked, "Father, how come? You said you wanted to die in the Holy Land and be buried in Jerusalem."

"Yes," answered the father, "to die—it's okay, but to live here?"

☺ ☺ ☺ ☺ ☺ ☺ ☺ ☺

Actual Personals That Appeared in Israeli Papers

Worried about in-law meddling? I'm an orphan. Write POB 74.

Yeshivah bochur, Torah scholar, long beard, payos. Seeks same in woman.

Desperately seeking shmoozing! Retired senior citizen desires female companion 70+ for kvetching (complaining) and krechtzing. Under 30 is also OK. POB 64.

Attractive Jewish woman, 35, college graduate, seeks successful Jewish Prince Charming to get me out of my parents' house. POB 46.

Divorced Jewish man, seeks partner to attend shul with, light Shabbos candles, celebrate holidays, build sukkah together, attend brisses (circumcisions), bar mitz-vahs. Religion not important. POB 658.

Nice Jewish guy, 38. No skeletons. No baggage. No personality. POB 78.

Female graduate student, studying kabbalah (Jewish mysticism), Zohar, exorcism of dybuks, seeks mensch. No weirdos, please. POB 56.

Staunch Jewish feminist, wears tzitzis (ritual fringes), seeking male who will accept my independence, although you probably will not. Oh, just forget it. POB 435.

Jewish businessman, 49, manufactures Sabbath candles, Chanukah candles, Havdalah candles, Yahrzeit candles. Seeks nonsmoker. POB 787.

Israeli professor, 41, with 18 years of teaching in my behind. Looking for American-born woman who speaks English very good. POB 555.

Couch potato latke, in search of the right applesauce. Let's try it for eight days. Who knows? POB 43.
80-year old bubby (grandma), no assets, seeks handsome, virile Jewish male, under 35. Object matrimony. I can dream, can't I. POB 545.

I am a sensitive Jewish prince whom you can open your heart to. Share your innermost thoughts and deepest secrets. Confide in me. I'll understand your insecurities. No fatties, please. POB 86.

Jewish male, 34, very successful, independent, self-made. Looking for girl whose father will hire me. POB 53.

☺ ☺ ☺ ☺ ☺ ☺ ☺ ☺

biggest Dobermans and Rottweilers. They developed a killing machine."

"Really?" the Israelis replied. "We had our top plastic surgeons working for five years to make an alligator look like a Dachshund!"

Chapter Two
Theology and God

Nearly every religion is based on the existence of God or some eternal power. In Judaism, the God idea is central. "Hear, O Israel, the Lord is our God, the Lord is One" has always represented the watchwords of the Jewish people. It should come as no surprise that God would enter Jewish humor. As the Psalmist himself states: The One who sits in Heaven shall laugh. Even God has a sense of humor. This chapter presents jokes of a theological nature, with God usually coming up with the funny punch line.

☺ ☺ ☺ ☺ ☺ ☺ ☺ ☺

A Modern Noah

In the year 2009, God came to Noah, who was now living in the United States, and said, "Once again, the earth has become wicked and overpopulated. and I see the end of all flesh before me. Build me another ark, and save two of every living thing along with a few good humans."

He gave Noah the blueprints, saying, "You have six months to build the ark before I will start the unending rain for forty days and forty nights."

Six months later God looked down and saw Noah weeping in his yard . . . but no ark.

"Noah," God roared. "I'm about to start the rain. Where is the ark?"

"Forgive me, God," begged Noah. "But things have changed. I needed a building permit. I've been arguing with the inspector about the need for a sprinkler system. My neighbors claim that I've violated the neighborhood zoning laws by building the ark in my yard and exceeding the height limitations. We had to go to the Development Appeal Board for a decision. Then the Department of Transportation demanded a bond be posted for the future costs of moving power lines and other overhead obstructions, to clear the passage for the ark's move to the sea. I argued that the sea would be coming to us, but they would hear nothing of it.

"Getting the wood was another problem. There's a ban on cutting local trees in order to save the spotted owl. I tried to convince the environmentalists that I needed the wood to save the owls. But no go.

"When I started gathering the animals, I got sued by an animal rights group. They insisted that I was confining wild animals against their will. As well, they argued the accommodation was too restrictive and it was cruel and inhumane to put so many animals in a confined space.

"Then the EPA ruled that I couldn't build the ark until they'd conducted an environmental impact study on your proposed flood.

"I'm still trying to resolve a complaint with the Human Rights Commission on how many minorities I'm supposed to hire for my building crew. Also, the trade unions say I can't use my sons. They insist I have to hire only union workers with ark building experience.

"To make matters worse, the IRS seized all my assets, claiming I'm trying to leave the country illegally with endangered species.

"So forgive me, God, but it would take at least ten years for me to finish this ark."

Suddenly the skies cleared, the sun began to shine, and a rainbow stretched across the sky.

Noah looked up in wonder and asked, "You mean, You're not going to destroy the world?"

"No," said God. "The government beat me to it."

☺ ☺ ☺ ☺ ☺ ☺ ☺ ☺

A Million a Second

Benjamin was walking through a forest pondering life. He walked, pondered, walked and pondered. He felt very close to nature and even close to God. He felt so close to God that he felt if he spoke, God would listen. So he asked, "God, are you listening?"

And God answered, "Yes."

Benjamin stopped and pondered some more. He looked towards the sky and said, "God, what is a million years to you?"

God replied, "Benjamin, a second to me is like a million years to you."

So Benjamin continued to walk and to ponder, walk and ponder. Then he looked to the sky again and said, "God, what is a million dollars to you?"

And God replied, "Benjamin, a penny to me is like a million dollars to you. It means almost nothing to me. It does not even have a value it is so little."

Benjamin looked down, pondered a little bit, and then looked up to the sky and said, "God, can I have a million dollars?"

God replied, "In a second."

☺ ☺ ☺ ☺ ☺ ☺ ☺ ☺

Lost in the Desert

A young man, Caleb, is lost and walking in the desert. One hot day, he spots an oasis of a rabbinical school. Tired and weak, he crawls up to its entrance and collapses.

A rabbi finds Caleb and calls the school doctor, who cares for his needs. Eventually, the doctor nurses him back to health. Feeling better and desiring to continue on his journey, Caleb asks the head rabbi for directions to the nearest town and if he could borrow one of the school horses.

The rabbi says, "Of course, you can borrow one of our horses, Caleb; just leave it in town at the local stable. They will return it. Also, there is a special thing about our horses at this school. You have to say 'Thank God' to make them go and 'Amen' to make them stop."

Not paying much attention, Caleb says, "Sure, okay."

So he gets on the horse and says, "Thank God" and the horse starts walking. Then he says, "Thank God, thank God" and the horse starts trotting. Feeling really brave, Caleb says, "Thank God" again and again until the horse takes off. Pretty soon, Caleb sees a cliff coming up and he does everything he can to make the horse stop.

"Whoa, stop, hold on!" Finally remembering what the head rabbi said, he shouts, "Amen." And the horse stops four inches from the edge of the cliff. Caleb wipes his brow, leans back in the saddle, takes a deep, long breath of air, thinking, "That was a close one." Then he says, "Thank God."

☺ ☺ ☺ ☺ ☺ ☺ ☺ ☺

God Calls the Pope

One day God called the Pope, and God said, "I have good news and bad news. First the good news. I'm tired of all the squabbling between the religions on earth. I have decided there will be only the one true religion."

The Pope was overjoyed and told God how wise His decision was, then asked, "So what's the bad news?"

God said, "The bad news is that I am calling from Jerusalem."

☺ ☺ ☺ ☺ ☺ ☺ ☺ ☺

Taking My Picture

A mother noticed that it was about time for school to dismiss and since it looked like it would rain, she drove toward the school to pick up her eight-year-old daughter. She turned down the street to see her daughter running towards her down the sidewalk. A bolt of lightning flashed, and the little girl looked up towards the sky, smiled, and then began running towards her mother's van.

Another lightning bolt flashed, and again the little girl looked towards the sky, smiled, and resumed running. This happened several more times until the little girl finally arrived at where her mother was parked.

Her mom immediately inquired as to the strange behavior. "Why did you keep stopping and smiling at the sky?" she asked her daughter.

"I had to, Mommy. God was taking my picture."

☺ ☺ ☺ ☺ ☺ ☺ ☺ ☺

Wayne the Painter

There was a tradesman, a painter called Wayne, who was very interested in making a penny where he could, so he would often thin down paint to make it go a wee bit further. As it happened, he got away with this for some time, but eventually the Baptist church decided to do a big restoration job on the painting of one of their biggest buildings. Wayne put in a bid, and because his price was so low, he got the job.

And so he set to erecting the trestles and setting up the planks and yes, I am sorry to say, thinning it down with turpentine.

Wayne was up on the scaffolding, painting away, the job nearly completed, when suddenly there was a horrendous clap of thunder, and the sky opened, the rain poured down, washing the thinned pain all over the church and knocking Wayne clear off the scaffold to land on the lawn among the gravestones, surrounded by telltale puddles of the thinned and useless paint.

Wayne was no fool. He knew this was a judgment from the Almighty, so he got on his knees and cried, "O God, forgive me. What should I do?"

And from the thunder a mighty voice spoke: "Repaint, repaint, and thin no more."

Theology and God

☺ ☺ ☺ ☺ ☺ ☺ ☺ ☺

On the Sixth Day

On the sixth day of creation, God turned to the angel Gabriel saying: "On this day I shall create a magic land. It shall be called Israel and will stand as holy. And its magnificence will be known all over the world. And I will choose to send to this land special people of goodness, intelligence, and conviction, so the land shall prosper. I shall call these inhabitants Jews."

"Pardon me, God," asked Gabriel, "but aren't you being too generous to these Jews?"

"Not really. Wait and see the neighbors I'm giving them."

☺ ☺ ☺ ☺ ☺ ☺ ☺ ☺

God Will Provide

A young woman brings home her fiancé to meet her parents. After dinner, the mother tells the father to find out about the young man. The father invites the fiancé to his study for a drink.

"So what are you plans?" the father asks the young man.

"I am a Torah scholar," he replies.

"A Torah scholar. Hmmmmm," the father says. "Admirable, but what will you do to provide a nice house for my daughter to live in, as she's accustomed to?"

"I will study," the young man replies, "and God will provide for us."

Continue →

25

"And how will you buy her a beautiful engagement ring, such as she deserves?" asks the father.

"I will concentrate on my studies," the young man replies. "God will provide for us."

"And children?" asks the father. "How will you support the children?"

"Don't worry, sir, God will provide," replies the fiancé.

The conversation proceeds like this, and each time the father questions, the young idealist insists that God will provide.

Later that evening the mother asks, "How did it go, honey?"

The father answers, "He has no job and no plans, but the good news is that he thinks I'm God."

☺ ☺ ☺ ☺ ☺ ☺ ☺ ☺

Heavenly Assistance

There was a man named Jacob who lived near a river in America. He was a very religious man. One day, the river rose over the banks and flooded the town, and Jacob was forced to climb onto his porch roof. While he was sitting there, a man in a boat came along and told Jacob to get in the boat. Jacob said, "No, that's okay, God will take care of me." So the man in the boat drove off.

The water rose, so Jacob climbed onto his roof. At that time, another boat came along, and the person in that one told Jacob to get in. He replied, "No, that's okay, God will take care of me." And the person in the boat left.

The water rose even higher, and Jacob climbed onto his chimney. Then a helicopter came and lowered a ladder. The man in the helicopter told Jacob to climb up the ladder and get in. He told the man, "That's okay." The pilot said, "Are you sure?" Jacob said, "Yeah, I'm sure. God will take care of me."

Finally, the water rose too high and Jacob drowned. He got up to heaven and spoke with the angel at the gate. Jacob questioned, "Why didn't God take care of me? What happened?"

The angel replied: "Well, He sent you two boats and a helicopter. What else did you want?"

☺   ☺   ☺   ☺   ☺   ☺   ☺   ☺

The Hadassah Ladies

A bus with fifty Hadassah Ladies turned over, and they were dispatched to heaven. Unfortunately, the computers were down, so God had to ask Satan to provide temporary housing. Soon after, God received an urgent telephone call from Satan telling him to take the women off his hands.

"What's the problem?" asked God.

Satan replied, "Those Hadassah Ladies are ruining my whole set up. Only two hours ago and already they raised $100,000 for an air conditioning system!"

☺   ☺   ☺   ☺   ☺   ☺   ☺   ☺

Jewish Survival

A new flood was predicted and nothing could prevent it. In three days, the waters would wipe out the world. The Dalai Lama appeared on worldwide media and pleaded with humanity to follow Buddhist teachings to find nirvana in the wake of the disaster.

The Pope issued a similar message saying, "It is still not too late to accept Jesus as your savior."

The chief rabbi of Jerusalem took a slightly different approach: "My people," he said, "we have three days to learn how to live under water."

Chapter Three
The Family

Jews have been called the "People of the Book," but they are just as surely the "people of the family." We began centuries ago as a family with Abraham, Isaac, Sarah, Rebekah, Rachel, Leah, and their children. Through the many difficult eras of Jewish history, strong family ties and a proliferation of children were not only a value. They also were a survival strategy. This chapter will focus on the Jewish family and its many challenges as portrayed in Jewish humor.

☺ ☺ ☺ ☺ ☺ ☺ ☺ ☺

The Michigan Greenberg Brothers

It was a sweltering day in August when the Greenberg brothers entered the posh Michigan offices of a notorious carmaker. Hyman Greenberg, the eldest of the three, announced, "We have an amazing invention that will revolutionize the automobile industry." The carmaker looked skeptical, but their threats to offer it to the competition kept his interest piqued. Hi Greenberg continued, "We would like to demonstrate it to you in person."

After a little cajoling, they brought the carmaker outside and asked him to enter a black car that was parked in front of the building. Norman Greenberg, the middle brother, opened the door of the car. "Please, step inside."

"What?" shouted the tycoon. "Are you crazy? It must be one hundred degrees in that car!"

"It is," smiled the youngest brother, Max, "but sit down and push the white button."

Intrigued, the tycoon pushed the button. All of a sudden a whoosh of freezing air started blowing from vents all around the car, and within seconds the automobile was not only comfortable, it also was quite cool!

"This is amazing," exclaimed the tycoon. "How much do you want for the patent?"

Norman spoke up, "The price is one million dollars." Then he paused. "And there is something else. We want the name Greenberg Brothers Air Conditioning to be stamped right next to your logo."

"Money is no problem," the car maker said, "but no way will I have a Jewish name next to my logo on my cars." They haggled back and forth for a while, and finally they settled. One and a half million dollars, and the name Greenberg would be left off. However, the first names of the Greenberg brothers would be forever emblazoned upon the console of every air conditioning system. And that is why today, whenever you enter a vehicle, you will see those three names clearly defined on the air conditioning control panel: NORM-HI-MAX.

☺ ☺ ☺ ☺ ☺ ☺ ☺ ☺

Oy, Yoy, Yoy
Three bubbes (Jewish grandmothers) sitting on a park bench. The first one lets out a heartfelt "Oy."

A few minutes later, the second bubbe sighs deeply and says, "Oy, vey."

A few minutes later, the third lady brushes away a tear and moans, "Oy, vey iz mir."

To which the first bubbe replies, "I thought we agreed we weren't going to talk about our children."

☺ ☺ ☺ ☺ ☺ ☺ ☺ ☺

What's a Name?

A young Jewish fellow develops a crush on a girl, but when he tells his father about her, the old boy just wants to know her family name. When the young guy tells him that the girl's name is Ford, the old boy tells him that Ford is not a good Jewish name, and he must forget her, and go and find a nice Jewish girl. So time passes, and the young guy finds another girl, but her name is Austin, so his father tells him the same thing—to find a nice Jewish girl with a nice Jewish name.

More time passes, and the young guy finds another girl, but this time he is sure that he has solved the problem because the girl's name is Goldberg.

"Goldberg! exclaims his father. "This makes me very happy because it is a real good Jewish name and from a good established family." Then he asks what her first name is.

"Is it one of my favorite names, like Rachel or Rebecca?"

"No, father," replied the young guy. "It's Whoopi."

☺ ☺ ☺ ☺ ☺ ☺ ☺ ☺

Election Day

The first Jewish president is elected. He calls his mother: "Mama, I've won the elections. You must come to the swearing-in ceremony."

"I don't know what to wear."

"Don't worry. I'll send you a dressmaker."

"But I only eat kosher food."

"Mama, I'm going to be the president. I can get you kosher food."

"But how will I get there?"

"I'll send a limo; just come, Mama."

"Okay, okay, if it makes you happy."

The great day comes and Mama is seated between the Supreme Court justices and the future cabinet members. She nudges the gentleman on her right: "You see that boy, the one with his hand on the Bible. His brother's a doctor."

☺ ☺ ☺ ☺ ☺ ☺ ☺ ☺

Tickets, Tickets

Mr. and Mrs. Greenberg go out to see *My Fair Lady* on stage. This is the most sold-out show of the year, and the scalpers are retiring on this one. Somehow, they've lucked into the front-row seats. But they notice that in the row behind them, there's an empty seat. When intermission comes, and none has sat in that seat, Mrs. Greenberg turns to the woman sitting next to it and asks, "Pardon me, but this is such a sold-out show, and in such demand. We were wondering why that seat is empty."

The woman said: "That's my late husband's seat."

Mrs. Greenberg is horrified and apologizes for being so insensitive.

But a few minutes later, she turns around again.

"Without meaning to be rude or anything, this is an incredibly hard show to get into. Surely you must have a friend or a relative who would have wanted to come and see the show?"

The woman nods, but explains, "They're all at the funeral."

☺ ☺ ☺ ☺ ☺ ☺ ☺ ☺

From the Other World

For months, Mrs. Pitzel had been nagging her husband to go with her to the séance parlor of Madame Freda. "Milty, she's a real gypsy, and she brings the voices of the dead from the other world. We can all talk to them. Last week, I talked with my mother, may she rest in peace. Milty, for twenty dollars you can talk to your zayde (grandpa) who you miss so much."

Milton Pitzel could not resist her appeal. At the very next séance at Madam Freda's Séance Parlor, Milty sat under the colored light at the green table, holding hands with the person on each side. All were humming, "Oooom, ooom, tonka tooom."

Madame Freda, her eyes lost in trance, was making passes over a crystal ball. "My medium . . . Vashtri," she called. "Come in. Who is that with you. Who? Mr. Pitzel. Milton Pitzel's zayde?"

Milty swallowed the lump in his throat and called, "Grandpa. Zayde?"

"Ah, Milteleh?" a thin voice quavered.

"Yes, yes," cried Milty. "This is your Milty. Zayde, are you happy in the other world?"

"Milteleh, I am in bliss. With your bubbe together, we laugh, we sing. We gaze upon the shining face of God."

A dozen more questions did Milty ask of zayde, and each question did his zayde answer, until "So now, Milteleh, I have to go. The angels are calling. Just one more question I can answer. Ask, ask."

"Zayde," sighed Milty, "when did you learn to speak English?"

☺ ☺ ☺ ☺ ☺ ☺ ☺ ☺

Play Parts

A little Jewish boy was telling his mother about how he had won a part in a play that was being done at school. His mother asked, "What is the part you will play, Saul?"

Saul answered, "I shall play the Jewish husband," to which the mother replied, "Well, you go right back to that teacher and tell her that you want a speaking part."

☺ ☺ ☺ ☺ ☺ ☺ ☺ ☺
Rogers 1-26-10

The Dating Game

It seems Yankel was pushing twenty-five and he'd never been on a date. His rosh yeshiva (headmaster of religious school) calls him into the office one day and says, "Yankel. Eighteen to the chuppah (wedding canopy). What's going to be already?"

The Family

Yankel blushes and explains to his rebbe that he grew up in a house full of brothers, and he's never even spoken to a girl anywhere near his age. He doesn't know what to say to girls. Besides, it would interrupt his learning. The rosh yeshivah puts a fatherly arm around him and tells him, "Don't worry about your learning. This is a *chiyuv* (obligation) with a capital *chet*. And as for what to say, you can talk about her family, you can talk about what she likes, and if all else fails you can talk philosophy."

Yankel leaves the rosh yeshiva repeating under his breath, "Family, likes philosophy. Family, likes philosophy. Family, likes philosophy." Finally, the day arrives and he goes out on his first date.

The young people sit down in the hotel lobby and look at one another uncomfortably. Yankel realizes that he's going to have to say something, and the first thing on the rosh yeshiva's list is family, so he blurts out: "Do you have any brothers?"

"No," replies the girl, and silence reigns.

Yankel thinks hard, and then comes up with, "Do you like baseball?"

"No" is the immediate reply.

Now Yankel is really at a loss. Ah, yes, philosophy. So Yankel leans forward and very intently, in his best talmudic tones, asks, "If you had a brother, would he like baseball?"

☺ ☺ ☺ ☺ ☺ ☺ ☺ ☺

Mother, Daughter, and the Big Wave

One day, a Jewish mother and her eight-year-old daughter were walking along the beach, just at the water's edge. Suddenly, a gigantic wave flashed up on the beach, sweeping the little girl out to sea.

"Oh, God, lamented the mother, turning her face toward heaven and shaking her fist. "This was my only baby. I can't have more children. She is the love and joy of my life. I have cherished every day that she's been with me. Give her back to me, and I'll go to the synagogue every day for the rest of my life."

Suddenly, another gigantic wave flashed up and deposited the girl back on the sand.

The mother looked up to heaven and said, "She had on a hat."

☺ ☺ ☺ ☺ ☺ ☺ ☺ ☺

Flying High

An elderly Jewish couple are sitting together on an airplane flying to the Far East. Over the public address system, the captain announces: "Ladies and gentlemen, I am afraid I have some very bad news. Our engines have ceased functioning, and this plane will be going down momentarily. Luckily, I see an island below us that should be able to accommodate our landing. Unluckily, this island appears to be uncharted. I am unable to find it on our maps. So the odds are that we will never be rescued and will have to live on the island for a very long time, if not for the rest of our lives."

The husband turns to his wife and asks, "Esther, did we turn off the stove?" Esther replies: "Of course."

"Esther, are our life insurance policies paid up?"

"Of course."

"Esther, did we pay our UJA pledge?"

"Oh, my God, I forgot to send the check."

"Thank heaven. They'll find us for sure!"

☺ ☺ ☺ ☺ ☺ ☺ ☺ ☺

Mother of All Diamonds

Sally is flying out to meet her boyfriend. She falls asleep on the plane and dreams about this gorgeous diamond ring he'll give her. When she opens her eyes, she spots an even bigger diamond on the finger of Mrs. Goldstein, a matron sitting next to her. This is the mother of all diamonds, and it is enormous, flawless, glittering.

"My, that's some diamond you've got there," Sally says. "I've never seen anything like it."

Mrs. Goldstein sighs. "I know, my child. This is no ordinary diamond. It's the famous Goldstein diamond. But it comes with a terrible curse."

"It does?" Sally moves to the edge of the seat. "So, what's the curse?"

Mrs. Goldstein sighs again. "Mr. Goldstein."

☺ ☺ ☺ ☺ ☺ ☺ ☺ ☺

How Do You Spell?

My son, Matt, a kindergartner, practices spelling with magnetic letters on the refrigerator: *cat*, *dog*, *dad*, and *mom* have been proudly displayed for all to see. One morning while getting ready for the day, Mitchell bound into the room with his arms outstretched. In his hands were three magnetic letters: G-O-D.

"Look what I spelled, Mom" Mitch exclaimed, a proud smile on his face.

"That's wonderful. I praised him." "Now go put them on the fridge so Dad can see when he gets home tonight." That religious education is certainly having an impact, I thought, happily.

Just then a little voice called from the kitchen. "Mom? How do you spell *zilla*?"

☺   ☺   ☺   ☺   ☺   ☺   ☺   ☺

The New Midrash
The Familiar Midrash (Legendary Story)

Once there were two brothers, each with a farm on the opposite side of the same hill. The first had a family. It came to be that, during the harvest, the first brother said to himself, "I have a wife, sons, and daughters to help during the harvest while my brother has no one to help." So late at night, he would sneak over the hill to his brother's farm and leave bags of grain.

Now, at about the same time, the second brother said to himself, "I live by myself whereas my brother has so many mouths to feed." So late at night, he would sneak over the hill to his brother's farm and leave bags of grain.

One night, they happened to run into each other, and each saw what the other was doing. They instantly realized what was happening, and hugged and kissed each other. And it is on that hill that the Temple was built.

☺ ☺ ☺ ☺ ☺ ☺ ☺ ☺

Updated Version

Once there were two brothers, each with a farm on the opposite side of the same hill. The first had a family—wife, sons, daughters. The second lived by himself. It came to be that, during the harvest, the first brother said to himself, "We have so many mouths to feed whereas my brother has only but himself." So late at night, he would sneak over the hill to his brother's farm and take bags of grain.

Now, at the same time, the second brother said to himself, "My brother has a wife, sons, and daughters to help during the harvest while I have no one to help." So late at night, he would sneak over the hill to his brother's farm and take bags of grain.

One night, they happened to run into each other and each saw what the other was doing. They instantly realized what was happening, and yelled at each other and beat each other up.

And it is on that hill that the Knesset (Israel's Parliament) was built.

☺ ☺ ☺ ☺ ☺ ☺ ☺ ☺

Rugalach: A Love Story

An elderly Jewish man lay dying in his bed. In death's agony he suddenly smelled the aroma of his favorite rugalach (rolled pastry) wafting up the stairs. He gathered his remaining strength and lifted himself from the bed. Leaning against the wall, he slowly made his way out of the bedroom and, with even greater effort, forced himself down the stairs, gripping the railing with both hands. With labored breath, he leaned against the doorframe, gazing into the kitchen.

Were it not for death's agony, he would have thought himself already in heaven. There, spread out on paper towels on the kitchen table, were literally hundreds of his favorite rugalach. Was it heaven? Or was it one final act of love from his devoted wife, seeing to it that he left this world a happy man?

Mustering one great final effort, he threw himself toward the table, landing on his knees in a rumpled posture. His parched lips parted. The wondrous taste of the pastry was already in his mouth, seemingly bringing him back to life.

The aged and withered hand, shaking, made its way to a piece at the edge of the table, when it was suddenly smacked with a spatula by his wife.

"Stay out of those," she said. "They're for after."

THE FUNERAL

☺ ☺ ☺ ☺ ☺ ☺ ☺ ☺

My Real Name

A young Jewish mother walks her son to the school bus corner on his first day of kindergarten.

"Behave, my bubeleh," she says. "Take good care of yourself and think about your mother, *tateleh* (little boy). And come right back home on the bus, *shein kindaleh*

(beautiful child). Your mommy loves you a lot, my *ket-saleh*" (little pussy cat).

At the end of the school day the bus comes back, and she runs to her son and hugs him.

"So what did my *pupaleh* (student) learn on his first day of school?"

The boy answers: "I learned by name is David."

☺   ☺   ☺   ☺   ☺   ☺   ☺   ☺

Four Jewish Brothers

Four Jewish brothers left home for college. They became successful doctors and lawyers, and prospered. Some years later, they chatted after having dinner together; they discussed the gifts that they were able to give to their elderly mother, who lived far away in another city. The first said, "I had a big house built for Mama." The second said: "I had a hundred-thousand-dollar theater built in the house." The third said, "I had my Mercedes dealer deliver her an SL600 with chauffeur."

The fourth said, "Listen to this. You know how mama loved reading the Torah. And you know, too, she can't read anymore because she can't see very well. I met this rabbi who told me about a parrot that can recite the entire Torah. It took twenty rabbis twelve years to teach him. I had to pledge to contribute $100,000 a year for twenty years to the temple. Let me tell you—it was worth it. All Mama has to do is name a chapter and verse and the parrot will recite it."

The other brothers were impressed. After the holidays mom sent out her thank-you notes. She wrote:

Milton: The house you built is so huge. I live in only one room, but I have to clean the whole house. Thanks anyway.

Marvin: I am too old to travel. I stay home; I have my groceries delivered, so I never use the Mercedes. And the driver you hired is a Nazi. The thought was good. Thanks.

Menachem: You give me an expensive theater with Dolby sounds; it could hold fifty people, but all my friends are dead. I've lost my hearing, and I'm nearly blind. I'll never use it. Thank you for the gesture just the same.

Dearest Melvin, You were the only son to have the good sense to give a little thought to your gift. The chicken was delicious. Thank you!

☺ ☺ ☺ ☺ ☺ ☺ ☺ ☺

The Thirty-Eight Days' Fast
A Jewish man calls his mother in Florida. "Mom, and how are you?"

"Not too good," says the mother. "I've been very weak."

The son says, "Why are you so weak?"

She says, "Because, I haven't eaten in thirty-eight days."

"Mama," the man says, "that's terrible. Why haven't you eaten in thirty-eight days?"

The mother answers: "Because I didn't want my mouth to be filled with food if you should call.

The Family

☺ ☺ ☺ ☺ ☺ ☺ ☺ ☺

The Prisoners

Two Jewish women were speaking about their sons, each of whom was placed in state prison. The first says: "Oy, my son has it so hard. He is locked away in maximum security; he never speaks to anyone or sees the light of day. He has no exercise and he lives a horrible life."

The second says: "Well, my son is in minimum security. He exercises every day; he spends time in the prison library, takes some classes, and writes home each week."

"Oy," says the first woman, "You must get such *nachas* (pleasure) from your son."

☺ ☺ ☺ ☺ ☺ ☺ ☺ ☺

Jewish Mother-in-Law Humor

Two Jewish women were sitting under hairdryers at the hairdresser. The first lady says, "So nu, how's your family?"

The second responds, "Oh, just fine. My daughter is married to the most wonderful man. She never has to cook—he always takes her out. She never has to clean—he got her a housekeeper. She never has to work—he's got such a good job. She never has to worry about the children—he got her a nanny."

She continues with a question to the first lady, "So how is your son these days?"

The first woman says, "Just awful. He is married to such a witch of a woman. She makes him take her out to dinner every night—she never cooks a dish. She made him get her a housekeeper. God forbid she should vacuum a carpet. He has to work like a dog, because she won't get a job, and she never takes care of their children, because she made him get her a nanny."

☺ ☺ ☺ ☺ ☺ ☺ ☺ ☺

A Good Laugh

The upset and concerned housewife Reena sprang to the phone when it rang and listened with relief to the kindly voice.

"Darling, how are you? This is Mama."

"Oh, Mama," she said, "I'm having a bad day." Breaking into bitter tears, she continued, "The baby won't eat, and the washing machine broke down. I haven't had a chance to go shopping, and besides, I've just sprained my ankle, and I have to hobble around. On top of that, the house is a mess, and I'm supposed to have the Goldbergs and Rosens for dinner tonight."

The voice on the other end said in sympathy, "Darling, let Mama handle it."

She continued, "Sit down, relax, and close your eyes. I'll be over in half an hour. I'll do your shopping, clean up the house, and cook your dinner for you. I'll feed the baby, and I'll call a repairman I know, who'll be at your house to fix the washing machine promptly. Now stop crying. I'll do everything. In fact, I'll even call your husband Morty at the office and tell him he ought to come home and help out for once."

"Morty?" said Rena. "Who's Morty?"

"Why, Morty's your husband. Is this 223-1374?"

Continued

46

"No, this is 223-1375."

"Oh, I'm sorry. I guess I have the wrong number."

There was a short pause, then Rena said, "Does this mean you're not coming over?"

☺ ☺ ☺ ☺ ☺ ☺ ☺ ☺

An Atheist's Proposal

Sarah comes home from her date, rather sad. She tells her mother, "David wants to marry me."

Her mother says, "David's such a good boy. So why such a sad face on my bubeleh?"

"Momma, David is an atheist. He doesn't even believe there's a hell."

Her mother says, "Bubeleh, marry him. Between the two of us, we can make him a believer."

6-29-10

☺ ☺ ☺ ☺ ☺ ☺ ☺ ☺

Jewish Mother Humor

Mona Lisa's Jewish Mother: "This you call a smile, after all the money your father and I spent on braces."

Christopher Columbus's Jewish Mother: "I don't care what you've discovered, you still should have written."

Michelangelo's Jewish Mother: "Why can't you paint on walls like other children? Do you know how hard it is to get this junk off the ceiling?"

Napoleon's Jewish Mother: "All right, if you're not hiding your report card inside your jacket, take your hand out of there and show me."

Continued ⟶

Abraham Lincoln's Jewish Mother: "Again with the hat. Why can't you wear a baseball cap like the other kids?"

George Washington's Jewish Mother: "Next time I catch you throwing money across the Potomac, you can kiss your allowance goodbye."

Albert Einstein's Jewish Mother: "But it's your senior photograph. Couldn't you have done something about your hair?"

Moses's Jewish Mother: "That's a good story. Now tell me where you've really been for the last forty years."

☺ ☺ ☺ ☺ ☺ ☺ ☺ ☺

Rogers
6-29-10

Falling in Love

A young Jewish man excitedly tells his mother he's fallen in love and is going to get married. He says, "Just for fun, Ma, I'm going to bring over three women and you try and guess which one I'm going to marry."

The mother agrees.

The next day, he brings three beautiful women into the house and sits them down on the couch and they chat for a while. He then says, "Okay, Ma. Guess which one I'm going to marry."

She immediately replies, "The redhead in the middle."

"That's amazing, Ma. You're right. How did you know?"

"I don't like her."

☺ ☺ ☺ ☺ ☺ ☺ ☺ ☺

Rogers
2-2-10
6-29-10
8-9-12

The Family

A Jewish Divorce

A Jewish parent calls his son in New York. The father says to David, "I hate to tell you, but your mother and I can't stand each other anymore, and we are divorcing. That's it. I want to live out the rest of my years in peace. I am telling you now, so you and your sister shouldn't go into shock later when I move out."

The father hangs up, and David immediately calls his sister in the Hamptons and tells her the news. The sister says, "I'll handle this."

The sister calls Florida and gets her father on the phone. She pleads to her father: "Don't do anything until David and I get there. We will be there Friday night."

The father says, "All right, all right already."

When the father hangs up the phone, he hollers to his wife "Okay, they're coming for Rosh Hashanah."

☺ ☺ ☺ ☺ ☺ ☺ ☺ ☺

Give Me the Manager

Jewish Mother: "Hello, Operator. Give me the manager from the fancy-dancy room service."

Manager: "Room Service."

Jewish Mother: "This is room 402, Mister Room Service. I vant to order breakfast."

Manager: "Certainly, Madam. What would you like?"

Jewish Mother: "For me, I vant a glass orange juice mit pits. The toast should be burned and—."

Manager: "Madam, I can't fill an order like that!"

Jewish Mother: "Aha! You did yesterday!"

Chapter Four
The Bible

The Bible is the oldest and most widely read book in our civilization. It has been in continuous circulation for almost 2,000 years and has been the source of religious ideals and values for countless millions of people. Ever since Sinai, the moral imperatives of the Five Books of Moses and the Prophets have provided great inspiration to social reformers and religious idealists. This chapter focuses on humor related to biblical themes.

☺ ☺ ☺ ☺ ☺ ☺ ☺ ☺

Bible Q & A Jokes

Q. Who was the greatest financier in the Bible?

A. Noah: He was floating his stock while everyone else was in liquidation.

Q. Who was the greatest female financier in the Bible?

A. Pharaoh's daughter: She went down to the bank of the Nile and drew out a little prophet.

Q. What kind of man was Boaz before he got married?

A. Ruth-less

Q. What kind of motor vehicles are in the Bible?

A. The Creator drove Adam and Eve out of the Garden in a Fury. David's Triumph was heard throughout the land.

Q. Who was the greatest comedian in the Bible?

53

A. Samson. He brought the house down.

Q. What excuse did Adam give to his children as to why he no longer lived in Eden?

A. Your mother ate us out of house and garden.

Q. Which servant of God was the most flagrant lawbreaker in the Bible?

A. Moses, because he broke all ten commandments at once.

Q. Where is the first tennis match mentioned in the Bible?

A. When Joseph served in Pharaoh's court.

Q. Which Bible character had no parents?

A. Joshua, son of Nun.

Q. Why didn't Noah go fishing?

A. He only had two worms.

Q. How do we know that they played cards in the ark?

A. Because Noah sat on the deck.

☺ ☺ ☺ ☺ ☺ ☺ ☺ ☺

Biblical Theme Songs

Adam and Eve: "Strangers in Paradise"
Methuselah: "Stayin' Alive"
Noah: "Raindrops Keep Falling on My Head"
Esther: "I Feel Pretty"
Moses: "The Wanderer"
Joshua: "Good Vibrations"
Esau: "Born to Be Wild"
Elijah: "Up, Up and Away"
Jezebel: "The Lady Is a Tramp"
Samson: "Hair"
Jonah: "Got a Whale of a Tale"

The Bible

Daniel: "The Lion Sleeps Tonight"
Shadrach, Meshach, and Abednego: "Great Balls of Fire"

☺ ☺ ☺ ☺ ☺ ☺ ☺ ☺

Adam's Problem in the Garden
Adam was walking through the Garden of Eden feeling very lonely, so God asked him: "What's wrong, Adam?"

Adam said he didn't have anyone to talk to.

God thought for a minute and then said that He was going to make him a companion and that it would be called Wonderful.

"Wonderful will gather food for you, cook for you, agree with your every decision, bear your children, never ask you to get up in the middle of the night to take care of them, never nag you, be the first to admit wrong when you've had a disagreement, and Wonderful never gives you a headache."

Adam inquired: "What will wonderful cost?"

God replied, "An arm and a leg."

Then Adam asked: "What can I get for a rib?"

☺ ☺ ☺ ☺ ☺ ☺ ☺ ☺

The Commandments
God goes to Italy and asks the citizenry, "Would you like to receive my Commandments?"

The Italians respond: "Give us a sample of what they contain."

When God says, "You shall not kill," they say, "Sorry, can't handle that, so we'll pass.

God goes to Spain and asks, "Would you like to receive my Commandments?"

The Spaniards respond: "Give us a sample of what they contain."

When God says, "You shall not steal," they say, "Sorry, can't handle that, so we'll pass."

God then goes to France and asks, "Would you like to receive my Commandments?"

The French respond, "Give us a sample of what they contain."

When God says, "You shall not commit adultery," they say, "Sorry, can't handle that, so we'll pass.

God goes to the Jews and asks, "Would you like to receive my Commandments?"

The Jews respond: "How much do they cost?"

When God answers, "They're free of charge," The Jews say, "Fine, we'll take ten!"

☺ ☺ ☺ ☺ ☺ ☺ ☺ ☺

Real Keeping Kosher
A dialogue while Moses is at the top of Mount Sinai.

God: "And remember Moses, in the laws of keeping kosher, never cook a calf in its mother's milk. It's cruel."

Moses: "Ohhhhhhhhh. So you are saying we should never eat milk and meat together."

God: "No, what I'm saying is, never cook a calf in its mother's milk."

Moses: "O God, forgive my ignorance. What you are saying is we should wait six hours after eating meat to eat milk products so the two are not in our stomachs.

God: "No, Moses, what I'm saying is, don't cook a calf in its mother's milk."

Moses: "O God, please don't strike me down for my stupidity. What you mean is we should have a separate set of dishes for milk and a separate set for meat and if we make a mistake we have to bury that dish outside—"

God: "Good lord Moses! Do whatever the heck you want!"

☺ ☺ ☺ ☺ ☺ ☺ ☺ ☺

Purim Bible Quiz

Q. What time of day was Adam created?
A. A little before Eve.
Q. What day in Adam's life was the longest?
A. The first. It had no Eve.
Q. Who in the Bible slept five in one bed?
A. David. He slept with his forefathers.
Q. Who was the straightest man in the Bible?
A. Joseph. Pharaoh made him ruler over Egypt.
Q. How do we know Joseph played tennis?
A. It says: Joseph served in the courts of Pharaoh.
Q. Where is baseball first mentioned in the Bible?
A. In the beginning (big inning)
Q. Where is baseball mentioned in the Book of Psalms?
A. Psalm 19: Who can understand his errors.

☺ ☺ ☺ ☺ ☺ ☺ ☺ ☺

Kids' Bible Statements

The following statements about the Bible were written by children and have not been retouched or corrected.

The seventh commandment is "thou shall not admit adultery."

Adam and Eve were created from an apple tree.

Noah's wife was called Joan of Ark.

Lot's wife was a pillar of salt by day, but a ball of fire by night.

Moses led the Hebrews to the Red Sea, where they made unleavened bread, which is bread without any ingredients.

The Egyptians were all drowned in the desert. Afterwards, Moses went up to Mount Cyanide to get the ten amendments.

Moses died before he ever reached Canada. Then Joshua led the Hebrews in the Battle of Geritol.

The greatest miracle in the Bible is when Joshua told his son to stand still and he obeyed him.

David was a Hebrew king skilled at playing the liar. He fought the Finkelsteins, a race of people who lived in Biblical times.

Solomon, one of David's sons, had 300 wives and 700 porcupines.

☺ ☺ ☺ ☺ ☺ ☺ ☺ ☺

If Purim Would Occur Today: Eight Ways

Following are ways the story of Purim would be different it if occurred today.

1. Story ends with Mordecai and Haman signing historic peace treaty on White House lawn.
2. Bigtan and Teresh caught trying to return rental van used in assassination attempt.
3. Haman's children finally killed by lethal injection after lengthy appeals process.
4. Jews required to drink until they no longer know the difference between Pat Buchanan and Al Sharpton.
5. In addition to *mishloach manot* (sending gifts) and *matanot l'evyonim* (gifts to the poor), Megillah institutes No Alternate-Side-of-the-Street-Parking.
6. Like Esther might never agree to marry one of those slimy Ayatollahs.
7. Instead of calling national fast day, rabbis hold ill-attended rally in front of Persian embassy.
8. Haman forced to share funds with rival extremist group Hezbollah.

☺ ☺ ☺ ☺ ☺ ☺ ☺ ☺

Elijah

The Sunday School teacher was carefully explaining the story of Elijah the Prophet and the false prophets of Baal. She explained how Elijah built the altar, put wood on it, cut the steer in pieces, and laid it upon the altar. And then Elijah commanded the people of God to fill four barrels of water and pour it over the altar. He had them do this four times.

"Now, said the teacher, "can anyone in the class tell me why God would have Elijah pour water over the steer on the altar?"

A little girl in the back of the room raised her hand with great enthusiasm, "To make the gravy," came her enthusiastic reply.

☺ ☺ ☺ ☺ ☺ ☺ ☺ ☺

Good News and Bad News

Moses was beginning to lose his patience while in Egypt. The Israelites were angry with him and even King Pharaoh began to give him the cold shoulder.

Suddenly, a loud voice shot from above: "You, Moses, now listen to me. I have for you good news and bad news."

Moses was shocked. And the loud voice continued: "Moses, you will lead the Israelites from Egyptian bondage. If Pharaoh refuses to release you from slavery, I will smite Egypt with a rainforest of frogs.

"You, Moses, will lead the Israelites to the Promised Land. If Pharaoh blocks your way, I will smite Egypt with a plague of grasshoppers.

"You, Moses, will lead the Israelites to the Promised Land. If Pharaoh blocks your way, I will smite Egypt with a plague of locusts.

"You, Moses, will lead the people of Israel to freedom and safety. If Pharaoh's army follows you, I will split the Red Sea and open your path to freedom."

Moses was totally stunned and stammered, "That's fantastic. I can't believe it. But what's the bad news?"

"You, Moses, must write the Environmental Impact Statement."

Chapter Five
Rabbis

There are many Jewish jokes that deal with incidents in the lives of rabbis, the religious leaders of the Jewish community. The rabbis of bygone years were known for their wisdom and their ability to decide questions of Jewish law. Because the new type of rabbi produced by modern life with its problems and complexities has shown himself as more efficient in a larger field of activities, there is an opportunity to create humorous situations in a variety of different areas.

☺   ☺   ☺   ☺   ☺   ☺   ☺   ☺

Seven Hearts

An old rabbi is talking with one of his friends and says with a warm smile, "I gladdened seven hearts today." "Seven hearts?" asks the friend. "How did you do that?" The rabbi strokes his beard and replies, "I performed three marriages." The friend looks at him quizzically. "Seven?" he asks. "I could understand six, but—"

"What do you think," says the rabbi, "that I do this for free?"

☺   ☺   ☺   ☺   ☺   ☺   ☺   ☺

The Rabbi's Hat

On a windy day in New York City a Hasidic rabbi's fur hat blew off and was rescued by a man who returned it to the rabbi. The rabbi said, "Thank you, are you Jewish?"

"No," said the man.

"Well," said the rabbi, "I can't bless you, but I see an afternoon of great wealth for you."

The man ponders, "What can it be? I know; I can make the last four races at the horse track." He goes and looks at the program and sees a horse named Top Hat in the next race. "An omen," he thinks, and bets $100 and wins. The next race has a horse named Stetson; again he bets and wins it all. The next race features a horse named Beret, and he naturally wins again. He bets it all on the next race and loses everything. He goes home and tells his wife the story.

"What horse did you bet on in the last race?" she asks.

He says, "Chateau—French for *hat*."

"Fool," she says, "*Chapeau* is French for *hat*. By the way, who won the race?"

"I don't know," he says, "some Japanese horse named Yomika" (skullcap).

☺ ☺ ☺ ☺ ☺ ☺ ☺ ☺

One Last Wish

Just before Rosh Hashanah a team of terrorists invades the shul and takes the rabbi, the cantor, and the shul president hostage. Hours later, the governor stands tough, he won't give them a million dollars, a getaway car, or a jumbo jet. The terrorists gather the three hostages in a corner and inform them that things look bad and they're going to have to shoot them. Nevertheless, to show that they're not really a bad bunch, they'll grant each hostage one single wish.

"Please," says the rabbi "for the last two months I've been working on my Rosh Hashanah sermon. What a waste to die now without having presented it before an audience. I'll go happily if you let me recite my sermon. It's an hour and ninety minutes long, tops." The terrorists promise to grant the wish.

"Please," says the cantor, "after fifty years I've finally gotten the 'Hineni' prayer just right. What a waste to die and not sing it to an audience. It's only about 45 minutes long, then I'll go happily. The terrorists promise to grant the cantor his wish, too, and they turn to the shul president.

"Please," says the president with tears in his eyes. "Shoot me first."

☺ ☺ ☺ ☺ ☺ ☺ ☺ ☺

The Shul Rabbi
The Shul rabbi told his congregation, "Next Shabbat I plan to speak about lying. To help everyone better understand my sermon, please read all sixty-six verses on the story of Laban in Genesis chapter thirty-three.

The following Sabbath, as the rabbi prepared to deliver his sermon, he asked for a show of hands from his congregation of how many members had read all sixty-six verses of Genesis chapter thirty-three. Almost every hand went up. The Rabbi smiled and said, "Genesis chapter thirty-three has only fifty-four verses. Now, let us get on with the discussion of the sin of lying."

☺ ☺ ☺ ☺ ☺ ☺ ☺ ☺

Good News and Bad News

The Good News, Rabbi: You converted seven people last week at the river.

The Bad News: You lost two of them in the swift current.

The Good News, Rabbi: The Sisterhood voted to send you a get-well card.

The Bad News: The vote passed by 31-30.

The Good News, Rabbi: The Board accepted your description the way you wrote it.

The Bad News: A search committee has been formed to find somebody capable of filling the position.

The Good News, Rabbi: The Board finally voted to add more congregational parking.

The Bad News: They are going to blacktop the front lawn of your house.

The Good News, Rabbi: Shabbat attendance rose dramatically the last three weeks.

The Bad News: You were sick.

The Good News, Rabbi: The Board wants to send you on a vacation.

The Bad News: Next year.

The Good News, Rabbi: Your biggest critic just left the congregation.

The Bad News: We offered him a position as head of the Board if he would return. He accepted!

☺ ☺ ☺ ☺ ☺ ☺ ☺ ☺

Lost and Found Wallet

A poor Jew finds a wallet with $700. At his shul he reads a notice stating that a wealthy Jew has lost his wallet and is offering a $50 reward to anyone who returns it. Quickly he locates the owner, giving him the wallet.

The rich man counts the money and says, "I see you have already taken your reward."

The poor man responds, "What are you talking about?"

The wealthy Jew continues, "This wallet had $750 in it when I lost it."

Both men present their case to the rabbi. The poor man first, then the wealthy man, who concludes by saying, "Rabbi, I trust you believe me."

The rabbi says, "Of course." The rich man smiles, and the poor man is devastated. Then the rabbi takes the wallet out of the wealthy man's hands and gives it to the poor man who found it.

"What are you doing?" the rich man yells angrily.

The rabbi responds, "You are, of course, an honest man, and if you say that you're missing wallet had $750 in it, I'm sure it did. But if the man who found this wallet is a liar and a thief, he wouldn't have returned it al all. Which means that this wallet must belong to somebody else. If that man steps forward, he'll get the money. Otherwise, it stays with the man who found it."

"What about the money?" the rich man asks.

"Well, we'll just have to wait until somebody finds a wallet with $750 in it!"

☺ ☺ ☺ ☺ ☺ ☺ ☺ ☺

Post Office
A rabbi arrived in a small town to raise funds for his yeshivah . He was scheduled to speak on Shabbat at the local synagogue the next day. He needed to mail a letter back home to his yeshivah with the collections he received to help pay the bills. As he walked down the street he saw several children playing together. They were Jewish, so he asked the little boy, "What's your name?"

He responded, "Michael."

Then the rabbi asked, "Michael, where is the post office?"

Michael said, "Three blocks down on your left side with the huge flagpole in the front."

The rabbi thought, What a smart child, as he thanked him adding, "Tomorrow I'll be speaking at the neighborhood shul. My sermon will be about making your home a Gan Eden (Garden of Eden). I hope to see you and your family."

Michael responded, "I don't think so, Rabbi, you don't even know your way to the post office."

☺ ☺ ☺ ☺ ☺ ☺ ☺ ☺

Rabbi on the Run
A rabbi is walking down the street one day when he sees a very small boy trying to press a doorbell on a house across the street. However, the boy is very short and the doorbell is too high for him to reach. After watching the boy's efforts for some time, the rabbi moves closer to the

boy's position and calls out to him, "Would you like some assistance?"

The little boy responds, "No."

The rabbi continues to watch as he crosses the street and walks up behind the little fellow. He places his hand kindly on the child's shoulder, leans over, and gives the doorbell a solid ring. Crouching down to the child's level, the rabbi smiles benevolently and asks, "Is there anything else I can help you with, my little man?"

To which the boy replies, "Yes, run like hell!"

☺   ☺   ☺   ☺   ☺   ☺   ☺   ☺

Three Chairs

The Orthodox rabbi meets three members of a Liberal congregation on the golf course and invites them to come to his synagogue on Shabbat. One hour after prayers begin, they show up. All the seats are filled. Already several men were seated on folding chairs. The rabbi whispers to the nearest man, "Jacob, please get three chairs for my Liberal friends in the back."

Jacob is hard of hearing so he leans closer and says, "I beg your pardon, Rabbi?"

The rabbi repeats his request: "Get three chairs for my Liberal friends in the back."

Jacob was still puzzled, but the service was just finishing, so he went to the front of the synagogue and loudly announced: "The rabbi says, 'Give three cheers for my Liberal friends in the back!"

☺ ☺ ☺ ☺ ☺ ☺ ☺ ☺

The Jewish Knight

When Rabbi Lerner was knighted by the Queen, as part of the knighting ceremony, he had to kneel before the Queen. And, as we all know, Jews do not bow before anyone except God. On top of that, he was told to recite a paragraph from the Christian liturgy during the actual knighting. The rabbi was in a quandary, as this was being televised, but he could not violate the Jewish laws.

The five honorees were lined up waiting for the Queen to receive them. As her royal highness entered the room, all kneeled, except for Rabbi Lerner. The Queen noticed this, but diplomatically ignored it. Then, the Queen began knighting each person. When she came to Rabbi Lerner, who still wasn't kneeling, she looked at him expectantly. Realizing she was waiting for the Latin recitation, he began to sweat and shake with nervousness. Then, in a fit of utter desperation, he said the first thing that came to mind: "Ma nishtannah ha-laylah ha-zeh!" (Why is this night different).

The Queen, perplexed, turned to the Prince and asked, "Why is this knight different from all other knights?"

☺ ☺ ☺ ☺ ☺ ☺ ☺ ☺

The Rabbi's Design

Bernie, a young Jewish boy, decided he wanted to be an aeronautical engineer and build airplanes. Over the years he studied diligently, went to the best schools, and finally got his degree. Soon he began to gain a reputation as the finest aeronautical engineer in all the land, so he decided to start his own company and build jets.

His company was such a hit that the president of the United States called Bernie into his office. "Bernie," the president said, "Israel wants to commission your company to build an advanced jet fighter for their country. You have our approval; go out and design the best jet fighter ever made."

Needless to say, Bernie was tremendously excited at this prospect. The entire resources of his company went into the building of the most advanced jet fighter in history. Everything looked wonderful on paper, but when they held the first test flight of the new jet, disaster struck. The wings couldn't take the strain and broke clean off the fuselage. The test pilot was able to parachute to safety.

Bernie was devastated. His company redesigned the jet fighter, but the same thing happened at the next test flight. The wings broke off once again. Now beside himself with great worry, Bernie went to synagogue to pray, to ask God where he had gone wrong. The rabbi saw Bernie's sadness, and naturally asked him what was the matter. Bernie then decided to pour out his heart to the rabbi.

After hearing the problem with the jet fighter, the rabbi put his hand on Bernie's shoulder and told him, "Listen, Bernie, I know how to solve your problem. All you have to do is drill a row of holes directly above and below where the wing meets the fuselage. If you do this, I absolutely guarantee the wings won't fall off."

Bernie just smiled and thanked the rabbi for his advice, but the more he thought about it, the more he realized he had nothing to lose. Maybe the rabbi had some holy insight. So Bernie did exactly what the rabbi told him to do. On the very next design of the jet fighter, they drilled a row of holes directly above and below where the wings met the fuselage. And it worked. The next test flight went perfectly.

Brimming with joyful glee, Bernie went to synagogue to tell the rabbi that his advice had worked. "Naturally," said the rabbi, "I never doubted it would."

"But Rabbi, how did you know that drilling the holes would prevent the wings from falling off?"

"Bernie," the rabbi retorted, "I'm an old man. I've lived for many years and I've celebrated Passover many, many times. And in all those years, not once, not once has the matzah broken on the perforation."

☺ ☺ ☺ ☺ ☺ ☺ ☺ ☺

The Chumash

A man had been in business for many years, and the business is going down the drain. He is seriously contemplating suicide, and he doesn't know what to do. So he goes to the rabbi to seek advice and tells his rabbi about all of his problems in the business. And he asks his rabbi what he would do.

The rabbi says, "Take a beach chair and a Bible, and put them in your car, and drive down to the edge of the ocean. Go to the water's edge. Take the beach chair out of the car, sit on it, and take the book out, and open it up.

72

The wind will ruffle the pages for a while, and eventually the Chumash (Bible) will stay open at a particular page. Read the first words your eyes fall on, and they will tell you what to do."

The man does as he is told. He takes a beach chair and a Bible and drives down to the beach. He sits on the chair at the water's edge and opens the Bible. The wind ruffles the pages of the Bible and then stops at a particular page. He looks down at the Bible and his eyes fall on words, which tell him what he has to do.

Three months later the man and his family come back to see the Rabbi. The man is wearing a one-thousand-dollar Italian suit. The wife is all decked out with a full-length mink coat, and the child is dressed in beautiful silk.

The man hands the rabbi a thick envelope and tells him that he wants to donate this money to the synagogue in order to thank the rabbi for his wonderful advice.

The rabbi is delighted. He asks him what words in the Chumash brought this good fortune to him.

The man replies, "Chapter 11."

☺ ☺ ☺ ☺ ☺ ☺ ☺ ☺

Kosher Rabbi

The Satmar rebbe has died. He goes straight up to heaven and finds a large table surrounded by a great number of long-bearded men studying Talmud and praying and swaying. On the table is a huge smorgasbord of delicacies: kishke, kugel, roast chicken, gefilte fish, and lots of other goodies. As the men learn and study, they take food off the table and eat it.

One man approaches the rebbe, "Rebbe, at last you have joined us. All day we study, and while we study, we have a great banquet. Please join us. Would you like something to eat?'

The rabbi looks at the man and asks him sternly, "Who's the mashgiach?" (rabbinic supervisor).

The man looks at the rebbe incredulously and replies, almost with a laugh, "This is the Garden of Eden. God is the mashgiach."

The rebbe strokes his long, white beard for an hour and ponders the matter. All his students look at him eagerly, waiting to hear the rebbe's reply.

Finally the rebbe speaks: "I'll have the fruit," he says, "on a paper plate."

☺ ☺ ☺ ☺ ☺ ☺ ☺ ☺

I Am Unworthy

Yizkor service, and the rabbi looking heavenward, passionately proclaims: "Dear God, I am but a speck on the ocean of Your countenance. I am nothing."

The cantor, seeing the rabbi, and not to be undone, chants: "Dear all-powerful God, among your unworthy flock, I am least worthy. I am nothing."

Finally, the shammash (sexton), being devout, looks skyward and utters: "Dear God, I am your lowliest servant, unworthy of your consideration. I am nothing."

Whereby the rabbi looks at the cantor with a smirk and whispers, "Now look who thinks he's nothing!"

The Visiting Rabbi

In the middle of his sermon, the visiting rabbi stopped and called the shammash (sexton). He pointed to a man in the fifth row.

"That man is sound asleep; go and wake him."

The shammash shook his head and said, "Wake him yourself, you put him to sleep."

☺ ☺ ☺ ☺ ☺ ☺ ☺ ☺

The New Rabbi

The synagogue in Toronto, Canada, had hired a new, young rabbi, only recently graduated from the seminary. The congregation adored him, except that he had one problem: his sermons were much too long.

One Friday night at services, in the middle of his usual long, extended sermon, the congregation was startled to hear the rabbi say: "It doesn't bother me much when now and then some of you look at your watches. But it bothers the heck out of me when I see you put your watches up to your ears to see if the things are still running."

☺ ☺ ☺ ☺ ☺ ☺ ☺ ☺

The New Tallis

The synagogue board was having a meeting about the rabbi's new contract. The president finally came out and said, "Rabbi, we can give you the new house, the new car, and the big raise, but we can't give you the new tallis" (prayer shawl).

The rabbi said, "What? You give me all those other things and can't give me a new tallis! Why?"

"Because," replied the president, "those fringe benefits will kill us."

☺   ☺   ☺   ☺   ☺   ☺   ☺   ☺

The Rabbi of Perfection

The results of a computerized survey indicate that the perfect rabbi preaches exactly fifteen minutes. He condemns sins, but never upsets anyone. He works from 8 a.m. until midnight and is also a janitor. He makes fifty dollars a week, wears good clothes, buys good books, drives a good car, and gives about fifty dollars weekly to the poor. He is fifty-eight years old and has preached thirty years. He has a burning desire to work with teenagers, and spends all his time with senior citizens. The perfect rabbi smiles all the time with a straight face, because he has a keen sense of humor that keeps him seriously dedicated to his work. He makes fifteen calls daily on congregants, shut-ins, and the hospitalized, and is always in his office when needed.

If your rabbi does not measure up, simply send this letter to six other synagogues that are tired of their rabbi, too. Then bundle up your rabbi, and send him to the synagogue on the top of the list. In one week, you will receive 1,643 rabbis and one of them will be perfect. Have faith in this procedure.

One congregation broke the chain and got its old rabbi back in less than three weeks.

Your servant,

_____

☺ ☺ ☺ ☺ ☺ ☺ ☺ ☺

Quakers

There was once a small Jewish population in an area that was dominated by Quakers. The Jews there had their own shul, and found their Quaker neighbors to be friendly. And in all, the two populations got on very well.

One summer, there was a terrible fire, and the synagogue was completely burned to the ground. The Jews were devastated, but they began raising money to build a new synagogue. The Quakers quickly saw their plight and also decided to lend a hand. They got together and had a meeting and decided that until the new synagogue could be built, the Jews should be able to pray in their church on Friday nights and Saturdays, since they only needed the church on Sundays. Furthermore, all funds placed in the tzedakah (charity) box would go toward the rebuilding of the synagogue. The Jews of the community, and their rabbi, were overwhelmed by the generous offer, and so it was.

All through the time of the building, the Jews prayed in the Quaker church on their Sabbath and the Quaker on theirs. As the months rolled by, the funds rolled in, and the synagogue came closer and closer to completion. Finally, just before Rosh Hashanah, the synagogue was ready to be re-opened. The rabbi decided that the first services would take place on the eve of Rosh Hashanah, and he announced this at the services in the Quaker church.

The whole community was outside the new synagogue for the grand festive re-opening. Everyone was congratulating each other as the rabbi went into the synagogue and walked up to the pulpit. He then had the gabbai (ritual assistant) open the doors for his congregants to enter.

After a few minutes the stream of people stopped, and the gabbai went up to the pulpit to inform the rabbi that everyone had been seated and the services could begin. The rabbi looked around and noticed something strange. He mentioned to the gabbai that there seemed to be several, if not many, congregants missing. To this, the gabbai replied: "I hate to tell you this, Rabbi, but you should know that some of your best Jews are Friends!"

☺ ☺ ☺ ☺ ☺ ☺ ☺ ☺

The Inexperienced Rebbe
The old rebbe died, and in the fashion of Chasidic custom, his very young son succeeded him as head of the community. Soon after, a group of disciples came to him and begged his intercession to end the drought and bring rain. The new rebbe did as he was asked, and his prayers were answered. The rain came, but unfortunately the heavens would not close. For days and days the rain poured down. The streets were impassable; homes were flooded; life had turned miserable. The same disciples came to the rebbe again and urgently pleaded for another miracle. They begged him to intercede once more with God so that the rains would stop. Again he did as requested. He prayed, but the rains did not stop. The rebbe's assistant explained to the disappointed disciples: "Our rebbe is still very inexperienced. He knows how to start the rain, but he hasn't learned yet how to make it stop."

Rabbis

☺ ☺ ☺ ☺ ☺ ☺ ☺ ☺

Life's Meaning

A much respected rabbi is at death's door. His students crowd around his bed, and one finally asks, "Rabbi, you have seen so much. Tell us, what is the meaning of life?"

"Life," the rabbi replies haltingly, "is a fountain."

The students clamor, "A fountain? What does that mean?"

"All right," the rabbi groans, "so it's not a fountain."

☺ ☺ ☺ ☺ ☺ ☺ ☺ ☺

Tax Returns

An IRS inspector walks into a shul and asks to see the rabbi. He is shown to the rabbi's office and is offered a seat.

"Rabbi, I believe a member of your synagogue, Mr. Klutz, states on his tax return that he has donated $100,000 to the synagogue. Tell me, Rabbi, is this correct?"

The rabbi answers, "Yes, he will."

☺ ☺ ☺ ☺ ☺ ☺ ☺ ☺

Divide and Conquer

A Jewish town had a shortage of men for wedding purposes, so they had to import men from other towns. One day a groom-to-be arrived on a train, and two mothers-in-law-to-be were waiting for him, each claiming ownership of him. A rabbi was called to solve the problem. After a few minutes of thought, he said: "If this is the situation—you both want the groom, we'll cut him in half, and give each one of you half of him."

To this replied one woman: "If that's the case, give him to the other woman."

The rabbi said: "Do that. The one willing to cut him in half is the real mother-in-law!"

☺   ☺   ☺   ☺   ☺   ☺   ☺   ☺

The Three Pious Men

Three Chasidim are each talking about who has the greatest rebbe. The first one says: "Our rebbe is so great, we were walking home from shul on Shabbat, and it was very hot. We said: 'Rebbe, it is so hot. What can we do?' The rebbe stopped and he prayed. And in front of the rebbe and behind the rebbe there was heat. And to the right of the rebbe and the left of the rebbe, there was heat. And in the area around the rebbe it became cool and fresh, and we all walked home."

The second one says: "That's nothing. We were walking home from shul one Shabbat, and it started to rain really hard. And we said, 'Rebbe, we're going to get sick. What should we do?' The rebbe stopped and prayed. And in front of the rebbe and behind the rebbe, there was rain. And to the right of the rebbe and to the left of the rebbe, there was rain. But in the area around the rebbe, there was no rain, and we all walked home."

The third said, "Is that all? We were walking home from shul on Shabbat, and we spotted a large bag filled with gold coins that was lying in the street. And we said, 'Rebbe, we could do so much work for the Chasidim, what should we do?' And the rebbe stopped and he prayed. And in front of the rebbe and behind the rebbe, there was Shabbat. . ."

☺ ☺ ☺ ☺ ☺ ☺ ☺ ☺

Four Rabbis
So it seems that these four rabbis had theological arguments, and they were always in accord against the fourth. One day, the odd rabbi out, after the usual "3 to 1 majority rules" statement that signified that he had lost again, decided to appeal to a higher authority. "O God," he cried. "I know in my heart that I am right and they are wrong. Please give me a sign to prove it to them."

It was a beautiful, sunny day. As soon as the rabbi finished his prayer, a storm cloud moved across the sky above the four. It rumbled once and dissolved. "A sign from God. See? I'm right. I knew it." But the other three disagreed, pointing out that storm clouds form on hot days.

So the rabbi prayed again. "O God. I need a bigger sign to show that I am right and they are wrong. So, please, God, a bigger sign." This time four storm clouds appeared, rushed toward each other to form one big cloud, and a bolt of lightning slammed into a tree on a nearby hill. "I told you I was right," cried the rabbi, but his friends insisted that nothing had happened that could not be explained by natural causes.

The rabbi is getting ready to ask for a "very big" sign, but just as he says "O God," the sky turns pitch black, the earth shakes, and a deep booming voice intones: "HEEEEEEEEEEEE'S RIIIIIIIIIIIIIIIGHT!"

The rabbi puts his hands on his hips, turns to the other three, and says, "Well?"

"So," shrugged one of the other rabbis, "now it's 3 to 2!"

☺ ☺ ☺ ☺ ☺ ☺ ☺ ☺

Rabbinic Argument
Two rabbis argued late into the night about the existence of God, and using strong arguments from the Scriptures, ended up indisputably disproving His existence. The next day, one rabbi was surprised to see the other walking into the shul for morning services.

"I thought we had agreed there was no God," he said.

"Yes, and what does that have to do with it?" replied the other.

☺ ☺ ☺ ☺ ☺ ☺ ☺ ☺

The Rabbis and the Squirrels
Two rabbis were discussing their problems with squirrels in their synagogue attic. One rabbi said they simply called an exterminator and they never saw the squirrels again. The other rabbi said, "We just gave them all a bar mitzvah, and never saw the squirrels again."

☺ ☺ ☺ ☺ ☺ ☺ ☺ ☺

The Golfing Rabbi
A Liberal rabbi was so compulsive a golfer that once, on Yom Kippur, he left the house early and went out for a quick nine holes by himself. An angel who happened to be looking on immediately notified his superiors that a grievous sin was being committed. On the sixth hole, God caused a mighty wind to take the ball directly from the tee to the cup—a miraculous shot. The angel was horrified. "A hole in one! he exclaimed. "You call this a punishment, Lord?"

Answered God with a sly smile, "So? Who can he tell?"

☺ ☺ ☺ ☺ ☺ ☺ ☺ ☺

The Rabbi Saves the Dog
One early winter morning, Rabbi Bloom was walking beside the canal when he saw a dog in the water, trying hard to stay afloat. It looked so sad and exhausted that Rabbi Bloom jumped in, and after a struggle, managed to bring it out alive.

A passerby who saw this remarked, "That was very brave of you. You must love animals. Are you a vet?"

Rabbi Bloom replied, "And uh, vat did you expect? Of course, I'm a vet! I'm a-freezing cold as vell!"

☺ ☺ ☺ ☺ ☺ ☺ ☺ ☺

The Rabbi and the Small House
A poor Jew turned to his rabbi for advice, "Rabbi, what shall we do? Our house is a hovel. It barely stands. We

have so many children. We fall on top of one another, and there is so little room for us."

The rabbi pondered the plight of the poor man, and said, "Bring your goat into the house." The poor man, astonished, nevertheless did as the rabbi advised.

The next day he returned, even more distressed. "Rabbi," he cried out. It's worse than ever before."

The rabbi solemnly intoned, "Bring all your chickens into the house." Again the poor man did as he was told, and on the following day returned to the rabbi, more desperate than ever.

"Rabbi," he cried, "Now there's no place for us to sit."

The rabbi smiled and said, "Good, now go home and chase out the goats and the chickens."

The poor man, still more confused, ran home and did as the rabbi commanded.

The next day he returned to the rabbi and thanked him profusely. "Rabbi, we have so much room now."

☺ ☺ ☺ ☺ ☺ ☺ ☺ ☺

The Rabbi and His Wife
The rabbi and his wife were cleaning up the house. The rabbi came across a box he didn't recognize. His wife told him to leave it alone—it was personal. One day, she was out and his curiosity got the better of him. He opened the box and inside he found 3 eggs and $2,000. When his wife came home, he admitted that he had opened the box and asked her to explain the contents to him. She told him, every time he had a bad sermon, she would put an egg in the box. He thought to himself, "In twenty years, only

three bad sermons, that's not bad." His wife continued, "And every time I got a dozen eggs, I would sell them for a dollar."

☺ ☺ ☺ ☺ ☺ ☺ ☺ ☺

The Gold Watch
Benny has stolen the rabbi's gold watch. He didn't feel good about it, so he decided after a sleepless night to go to the rabbi.

"Rabbi," I stole a gold watch."

"But Benny, that's forbidden. You should return it immediately."

"What shall I do?"

"Give it back to the owner."

"Do you want it?"

"No, I said return it to its owner."

"But he doesn't want it."

"In that case, you can keep it."

☺ ☺ ☺ ☺ ☺ ☺ ☺ ☺

Rabbi in Heaven
A rabbi dies and goes up to the gates of heaven. Before he's let in, the angel in charge has to consult with God for a long time whether he deserves a place in heaven. As the rabbi is waiting, an Israeli bus driver approaches the gates of heaven. Without a second thought, the angel who was consulting with God lets the bus driver through. The rabbi points at the bus driver and yells, "Hey! Why does

he get in so quickly? He's a simple bus driver, while I'm a rabbi."

The angel explains, "Dear rabbi, you don't understand. When you would be giving your sermon during the prayer services, your whole congregation would fall asleep. When this bus driver drove towards Tel Aviv, all his passengers would be at the edge of their seats, praying to God."

☺ ☺ ☺ ☺ ☺ ☺ ☺ ☺

Last Wishes
A woman in Brooklyn decided to prepare her will and make her final requests. She told her rabbi she had two final requests. First, she wanted to be cremated; second, she wanted her ashes scattered all over the shopping mall.

"Why the shopping mall?" asked the rabbi.

"Then I'll be sure my daughters visit me twice a week."

☺ ☺ ☺ ☺ ☺ ☺ ☺ ☺

The Pilot's Wish
Thirteen rabbis were on a flight from New York to Jerusalem when the super jet they were flying on experienced a great storm. One of the rabbis called the stewardess with the intention of calming her nerves. He said, "Tell the pilot that everything will be all right because there are thirteen very religious men about the jet."

A little later the stewardess returned from the cockpit with a message from the pilot to the head rabbi. "He said he was glad to know that we have thirteen holy men aboard this super jet, but he would rather just have one good engine."

☺   ☺   ☺   ☺   ☺   ☺   ☺   ☺

Prayer for Rain

A severe drought had a disastrous effect on the crops, and unless rain fell, the farmers would suffer great losses. To demonstrate the power of prayer, the rabbi decided to use the approaching festival of Shemini Atzeret, when it is customary to recite the prayer for rain. To this end, he engaged a cantor to officiate for the festival.

On the holy day, the rabbi preached a soul-stirring sermon. He urged his congregants to worship fervently for a favorable response to prayer for rain. With deep emotion the cantor chanted the special prayer for rain.

It was not surprising that a heavy rain fell as service were concluded. So abundant was the rain that it seems the heavens themselves were emptying. Surely the rabbi was being vindicated as their prayers were answered.

However, whatever had been left of the crops was completely destroyed by the plethora of water. Two neighbors who had left their houses in the rain to examine their ruined fields met on the road. With a sigh of anguish, one said to the other: "The rabbi really knows how to get answers to his prayers."

The other retorted: "That is quite true, but he certainly doesn't know how to irrigate a field."

☺ ☺ ☺ ☺ ☺ ☺ ☺ ☺

The "Limited" Rabbi

A rabbi of limited abilities, but possessed of unlimited ego, hoped to advance his career by writing. He assembled a collection of his sermons and brought it to a famous scholar to seek his endorsement. The scholar agreed to examine it. After perusing several pages, he came to the conclusion that it was a work of no merit.

Not wishing to hurt the writer's feelings, he took a sheet of paper and wrote at the top, "I heartily recommend this worthwhile book." At the bottom of the paper, he signed his name, leaving a large empty space in between.

The rabbi read his comments and was both elated and confused. He asked: "Why did you leave so much empty space between your words of praise and your signature?"

The scholar replied, "I did so to fulfill the Torah's commandment, 'You shall keep far from any untruth'" (Exodus 23:7).

☺ ☺ ☺ ☺ ☺ ☺ ☺ ☺

The Departed Soul

A certain person claimed that his father's departed soul returned to this world every Sabbath and attended Sabbath services. Every week, he would call his father to the Torah, listening attentively to what he claimed was the faint sound of his father's blessing.

When word of this reached the ears of Rabbi Yaakov Sender, he smiled and said, "Next week, tell him to give his father hagbah (honor of lifting the Torah).

☺ ☺ ☺ ☺ ☺ ☺ ☺ ☺

The Telephone Call
Mendy telephones Rabbi Twersky and says, "Rabbi, I know tonight is Yom Kippur, but tonight is the World Series, and the Yankees are playing. Rabbi, I've been a Yankee fan all of my life. I've just got to watch the Yankees game on TV.

Rabbi Twersky replies, "Mendy, that's what video recorders are for."

☺ ☺ ☺ ☺ ☺ ☺ ☺ ☺

Godspeed
The man sitting on the park bench facing the synagogue was a picture of dejection. His shabby clothes looked as if he had slept in them, and his tired face was covered by a heavy growth. Overcome by pity for the derelict, the rabbi pressed a five-dollar bill into his hand, whispered "Godspeed," and was gone. A few hours later the stranger burst into the rabbi's study and with obvious delight, threw a fistful of dollars on the rabbi's desk.

"Rabbi," he exclaimed, "Godspeed paid fourteen to one!"

1-26-10
Roger

☺ ☺ ☺ ☺ ☺ ☺ ☺ ☺

Sacrifice of Isaac

Abraham the first patriarch wants to upgrade his PC to Windows 95. Isaac his son is incredulous. "Dad," he says, "you can't run Windows 95 on your old, slow 386. Everyone knows that you need at least a fast 486 with a minimum of 16 megs of memory in order to multitask effectively with Windows 95."

But Abraham, the man of extreme faith, gazes calmly at his son and replies, "God will provide the RAM my son."

☺ ☺ ☺ ☺ ☺ ☺ ☺ ☺

Three Chasidim

Three Chasidim chanced to meet at an inn. Naturally, their conversation turned to stories about their rebbes. The first one said, "My rebbe, long may he live, is so meticulous about observing our dietary laws that he insists on having two cooks in his home, one to prepare all the meat meals, and the other one to prepare all the dairy meals.

The second said, "My rebbe, long may he live, is even stricter. If he eats meat, he doesn't wait the customary six hours before tasting anything dairy; he waits an entire day."

The third Chassid, not to be outdone by the first two, said, "My rebbe, long may he live, is even stricter than that. If he is studying in the holy books the chapters concerning the preparation of meat dishes, he waits a full day before turning to the chapters about dairy foods."

☺ ☺ ☺ ☺ ☺ ☺ ☺ ☺

A Great Sleep

A Chasid told the story about his rebbe: "All day long he busies himself with the study of holy books. And all night long he devotes himself to the needs of his followers."

A listener asked, "If that be the case, when does your rebbe sleep?"

He replied, "Our rebbe sleeps for only one hour, just before the morning prayers."

"But," his questioner continued, "how can he manage on only one hour of sleep?"

The proud Chasid answered, "My rebbe is a great maker of miracles. He can sleep more in one hour than someone who sleeps the whole night."

☺ ☺ ☺ ☺ ☺ ☺ ☺ ☺

A Cantor's Prayer

At the Shemini Atzeret services, the cantor exploited every word of the prayer for rain in order to display his vocal abilities. No sooner was the prayer finished than there was a deluge of rain.

After the service the cantor bragged to the rabbi: "I am pleased that God listened to my prayer, and that I caused rain to fall."

The rabbi quickly retorted, "I'm not at all surprised. Some time ago people like you caused the flood."

☺ ☺ ☺ ☺ ☺ ☺ ☺ ☺

The Big Concern

Several days before Passover a poor man came to the rabbi for advice. "Rabbi, he complained, "I'm in dire circumstances. Passover is almost here, but I do not have the means to properly observe it. I must get money for matzah and wine and meat. And we don't have festive clothing for the holiday either."

The rabbi tried to soothe them. "Don't worry," he said. God will help you."

But the unhappy man would not be comforted.

"I've too many worries, Rabbi," he wailed, "I'm afraid they're too much for me."

"In that case," said the rabbi, "let's see what your needs are." And he began to figure.

"How much do you need for food?"

"Fifteen rubles."

"Clothes for the children."

"Twenty rubles."

"A new dress for your wife?"

"Eight rubles."

"A new suit for yourself?"

"Ten rubles."

The rabbi then added up the total of the various items and said, "You need altogether fifty-three rubles. Now at least you won't have to worry about matzah, meat, wine and clothing; you'll have only one worry—where to get the fifty-three rubles!"

☺ ☺ ☺ ☺ ☺ ☺ ☺ ☺

The Open-Minded Rabbi

There was once a rabbi who was so open-minded that he was able to see every side of a question. One day a man came to see him with the request that he grant him a divorce.

"What do you hold against your wife?" asked the rabbi gravely.

The man went into a lengthy recital of his complaints.

"You are right," he agreed when the man finished.

Then the rabbi turned his attention to the woman.

"Now let me hear your story, "he said.

And the woman in her turn began to tell him of the cruel mistreatment she had suffered at the hands of her husband.

The rabbi listened with obvious distress. "You are right," he said with conviction when she finished.

At this, the rabbi's wife, who was present, exclaimed: "How could this be? Surely both of them couldn't be right."

The rabbi reflected. "You're right, too," he agreed.

☺   ☺   ☺   ☺   ☺   ☺   ☺   ☺

The Cow that Fell into the Lake

One Sabbath, Beryl stood at the window in his rabbi's study looking outside.

"Rabbi," he asked, "If someone sees a cow drowning on the Sabbath, must one save it or let it drown?"

"Of course, you can't save it. It's not permissible. What are you looking at anyhow?"

"Nothing. A cow fell into the lake."

"What can one do?" said the rabbi. "The Torah forbids it."

"Just take a look. The water is now going over her head. It's a pity, but she's going to drown."

"What can one do?"

"So, Rabbi, nothing can be done?"

"What is your concern anyway?"

"Now I can no longer see her. What a pity."

"What's the matter with you Beryl? Why are you so troubled?"

"You'll be sorry, Rabbi. I tell you—you'll truly be sorry."

"Why in God's name will I be sorry?"

"Rabbi, it's your cow!"

☺ ☺ ☺ ☺ ☺ ☺ ☺ ☺

The Problem

A man is having a problem with his son and goes to see his rabbi. "I sent him to Hebrew school and gave him a very expensive bar mitzvah," says the man, "and now he tells me he's decided to become a Christian. Rabbi, where did I go wrong?"

"Funny you should come to me," said the rabbi. "I also brought my boy up in the faith and gave him a fancy bar mitzvah. Then one day, he, too, tells me he's decided to become a Christian."

"So what did you do?" asked the man.

"I turned to God for the answer," replied the rabbi.

"And what did He say?" said the man.

"God said: 'Funny, you should come to me—'"

Rabbis

☺ ☺ ☺ ☺ ☺ ☺ ☺ ☺

The Upset Rabbi

A rabbi who has been leading a congregation for many years is upset by the fact that he's never been able to eat pork. So he creates a plan whereby he flies to a remote tropical island and checks into a hotel. He immediately gets himself a table at the finest restaurant and orders the most expensive pork dish on the menu. As he's eagerly waiting for it to be served, he hears his name called from across the restaurant. He looks up to see five of his most loyal congregants approaching.

His luck, they'd chosen the same time to visit the same remote location. Just at that moment, the waiter comes out with a huger silver tray carrying a gigantic roasted pig with an apple in its mouth.

The rabbi looks up sheepishly at his congregants and says, "Wow, you order a baked apple and look how it's served!"

☺ ☺ ☺ ☺ ☺ ☺ ☺ ☺

The Good Marriage

When a Jewish couple was celebrating their fiftieth anniversary at the temple's marriage marathon, the rabbi asked Saul to take a few minutes to share some insight into how he managed to live with the same woman all these years.

The husband replied to the audience, "Well, I treated her with respect, spent money on her, but mostly I took her traveling on special occasions."

Rogers
11-23-10

The rabbi inquired, "Trips to where?"

"For our twenty-fifth anniversary, I took her to Beijing, China."

The rabbi then asked, "What a terrific example you are to all husbands, Saul. Now please tell the audience what you're going to do for your wife on your fiftieth anniversary?"

Saul replied, "I'm going to go get her and bring her home!"

8-17-12

☺ ☺ ☺ ☺ ☺ ☺ ☺ ☺

The Prayer

A rabbi was talking to a precocious six-year-old Mendel. "So you tell me that your mother says prayers for you each night. That's most commendable. What does she actually say?"

Little Mendel replied, "Thank God he's in bed!"

☺ ☺ ☺ ☺ ☺ ☺ ☺ ☺

Here is a sampling of jokes involving a rabbi and a member of the clergy of another faith. In all of these humorous situations, there is a dilemma or question to be solved, with the rabbi always coming up with the humorous punch line.

☺ ☺ ☺ ☺ ☺ ☺ ☺ ☺

The Rabbi, Pope, and Telephone

The chief rabbi of Israel and the Pope are meeting in Rome. The chief rabbi notices an unusually fancy phone on a sidetable in the Pope's private chambers. "What is that phone for?" he asks the pontiff.

"It's my direct line to God." The chief rabbi is skeptical and the Pope notices. The Holy Father insists the rabbi try it out, and indeed, he is connected to the Lord. The rabbi holds a lengthy discussion with Him.

After hanging up, the rabbi says, "Thank you very much. This is great. But listen, I want to pay for my phone charges." The Pope, of course, refuses, but the rabbi is steadfast, and finally, the pontiff gives in. He checks the counter on the phone and says, "All right. The charges were 100,000 shekels." The chief rabbi gladly hands over the payment.

A few months later, the Pope is in Jerusalem on an official visit. In the chief rabbi's chambers, he sees a phone identical to his and learns it, too, is a direct line to God. The Pope remembers he has an urgent matter that requires divine consultation and asks if he can use the rabbi's phone. The rabbi gladly agrees, hands him the phone, and the Pope chats away.

After hanging up, the Pope offers to pay for the phone charges. Of course, the chief rabbi refuses to accept payment. After the Pope insists, the rabbi relents and looks on the phone counter. Fifty shekels.

The Pope looks surprised, "Why so cheap?"

The rabbi smiles, "Local call."

☺ ☺ ☺ ☺ ☺ ☺ ☺ ☺

Charity Begins at Home

A priest, a minister, and a rabbi were sitting around wondering what to do with all the money they collected from charity. The priest said: "I got an idea. Let's draw a circle, throw all the money up in the air, and what falls in the circle we give to God."

The minister said: "I got a better idea. Let's draw a circle, throw all the money up in the air, and what falls outside the circle, we give to God."

The rabbi said: "I got even a better idea. Let's draw a circle, throw all the money up in the air, and let God take what he wants, and what falls to the ground, we keep."

☺ ☺ ☺ ☺ ☺ ☺ ☺ ☺

A Religious Accident

A rabbi and a priest are driving separate cars on a mountain road during a very bad snowstorm. The priest is driving down the mountain. The rabbi is driving up the mountain. They meet on a narrow curve in the road. Their cars crash. The priest's car goes down over the hillside and smacks into a large pine tree. The rabbi's car crashes into the side of the mountain. Both cars are seriously damaged.

The rabbi is not hurt. He climbs out of his tangled mess, runs down the hillside, and finds the priest slumped over the steering wheel. The rabbi says, "Father, are you hurt? Are you all right?"

The priest regains consciousness, and responds, "I'm okay."

The rabbi then asks, "Would you like a small shot of whiskey?"

The priest responds, "That would be nice."

The rabbi hurries up the hill, goes to the glove box of his car, takes out a small silver flask of whiskey, and then returns to the priest. He offers him a drink. The priest takes one generous swig, then hands the bottle to the rabbi, who says, "Please take one more. You're in such pain."

The priest obliges. Then after the second drink, the priest offers the flask to the rabbi, who again declines, insisting there isn't much and he should take one more drink. After the third drink, the priest asks the rabbi, "Aren't you going to have a drink with me?"

The rabbi takes the flask, immediately puts the cap on it, and hands it back to the priest, and responds, "I'll have a drink after the police arrive."

☺ ☺ ☺ ☺ ☺ ☺ ☺ ☺

The Accident

A rabbi and a priest get into a car accident. It seems the priest was going at a rapid rate and smashed into the rabbi. Along comes a cop, who says in his Irish brogue, "Now Father, tell me, how fast was the rabbi backing up when he hit you?"

☺ ☺ ☺ ☺ ☺ ☺ ☺ ☺

After They Die

A Catholic priest, a Protestant minister, and a rabbi are discussing what they would like people to say after they die and their bodies are put on display in open caskets.

Priest: "I would like someone to say: 'He was a good man, an honest and generous man.'"

Minister: "I would like someone to say: 'He was very kind and fair, and he was very good to his parishioners.'"

Rabbi: "I would want someone to say, 'Look, he's moving!'"

☺ ☺ ☺ ☺ ☺ ☺ ☺ ☺

What's for Dinner?

The main course at the big civic dinner was baked ham with glazed sweet potato. Rabbi Cohen regretfully shook his head when the platter was passed to him.

"When," scolded Father Kelly playfully, "are you going to forget that silly rule of yours and eat ham like the rest of us?"

Without skipping a beat, Rabbi Cohen replied: "At your wedding reception, Father Kelly."

☺ ☺ ☺ ☺ ☺ ☺ ☺ ☺

The Monk, the Priest, and the Rabbi

A Buddhist monk goes to a barber to have his head shaved. "What should I pay you?" the monk asks. "No price, for a holy man such as yourself," the barber answers. And what do you know, the next day the barber comes to open his shop and finds on his doorstep a dozen gemstones.

That day, a priest comes in to have his haircut. "What shall I pay you, my son?" "No price, for a man of the cloth such as yourself." And what do you know, the next day the barber comes to open his shop, and finds on his doorstep a dozen roses.

That day, Rabbi Finkelstein comes in to get his *peyos* (sideburns) trimmed. "What do you want I should pay you?" "Nothing, for a man of God such as yourself." And the next morning, what do you know. The barber finds on his doorstep—a dozen rabbis!

☺ ☺ ☺ ☺ ☺ ☺ ☺ ☺

Jewish Heaven

A minister told his friend Rabbi Berg, "Last night I dreamed of the Jewish heaven. It was a slum, and it was overflowing with people—running, playing, talking, sitting—doing all sorts of things. But the dream, and the noise, was so terrific that I woke up."

The rabbi said: "Really? Last night I dreamed of the Protestant heaven. It was a nice proper suburb, with neatly trimmed lawns, and houses all neatly lined up."

"And how did the people behave?" asked the minister.

"What people?"

☺ ☺ ☺ ☺ ☺ ☺ ☺ ☺

A Proposal

The Pope met with his cardinals to discuss a proposal from Benjamin Netanyahu, the prime minister of Israel.

"Your Holiness," said one of his cardinals. "Mr. Netanyahu wants to challenge you to a golf game to show the friendship and spirit shared by the Jewish and Catholic faiths."

The Pope thought this was a great idea, but he had never golfed in his life. "Don't we have a cardinal to represent me?" he asked.

"None that plays very well," a cardinal replied. "But," he added, there is a man named Arnold Palmer, an American golfer who is a devout Catholic. We can offer to make him a cardinal, then ask him to play Mr. Netanyahu as your personal representative. In addition, to showing our spirit of cooperation, we'll also win the match."

Everybody agreed it was a fantastic idea. The call was made and Arnold Palmer accepted and agreed to play. The day after the golf match, Palmer reported to the Vatican to inform the Pope of the result. "I have some good news and bad news, your Holiness," said Palmer.

"Tell me the good news first, Cardinal Palmer," said the Pope.

"Well, your Holiness, I don't enjoy bragging, but even though I've played some pretty amazing rounds of golf in my life, this was the best I have every played. I must have been inspired from above. My drives were long and straight, and my putting was true and directed. With all due respect, my play was nothing short of miraculous."

"And there's bad news?" asks the Pope.

"Yes," Palmer replied." I lost to Rabbi Tiger Woods by four strokes!"

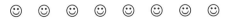

Three Friends

Three friends, a priest, pastor, and a rabbi, celebrated the twenty-fifth anniversary of their weekly card game by booking passage on a cruise ship. They were well aware that the ship's captain forbade all forms of gambling on board the vessel. Undeterred, the three clergymen passed their time at sea gambling in their stateroom. Word reached the captain who summoned them to his quarters. "It's been reported to me that you have been gambling," he said to them. Eyeing the priest, he said in a stern voice, "Father, you surely would not tell an untruth. Were you gambling?" The priest denied that he had been gambling.

The captain turned to the pastor, "I know that you are an honorable man of the Lord and will not lie. Were you and the others gambling?" The pastor calmly denied that any gambling had occurred.

Turning to the last of the three men, the captain continued, "Rabbi, surely you would not speak falsehood. Were you gambling?" With a look of innocence, the rabbi answered, "With whom?"

Chapter Six
Humor from Chelm

A very popular humorous tradition from Eastern Europe involves tales of the people of Chelm, a town reputed in these jokes to be inhabited by fools (including their rabbi). These jokes were usually focused on silly solutions to problems. Some of these solutions would display foolish wisdom, in which the correct answer was reached by the wrong train of reasoning, while others were simply wrong. Authors such as Sholom Aleichem and Isaac Bashevis Singer told many of the Chelm tales. This chapter offers some examples of typical Chelmite humor.

☺ ☺ ☺ ☺ ☺ ☺ ☺ ☺

Snow in Chelm

In Chelm, the shammash (sexton) used to go around getting everyone up for morning worship. Each time that it snowed, the people would complain that although the snow was beautiful, they could not see it in its pristine state because by the time they got up in the morning, the shammash had already trekked through the snow. So the townspeople decided that they had to find a way to be awakened for minyan, without having the shammash making track marks in the snow.

Finally, the people of Chelm hit on a solution. They got four volunteers to carry the shammash around on a table when there was fresh snow in the morning. That way, the shammash could make his wakeup calls, but he would not leave tracks in the snow.

☺ ☺ ☺ ☺ ☺ ☺ ☺ ☺

Building a Synagogue
The town of Chelm decided to build a new synagogue. So, some strong able-bodied men were sent to a mountaintop to gather heavy stones for the foundation. The men put the stones on their shoulders and trudged down the mountain to the town below. When they finally arrived, the town constable screamed, "Foolish me. You should have rolled the stones down the mountain."

The men agreed that this was a fine idea. So they turned around, and with the stones still on their shoulders, they trudged back up the mountain, and rolled the stones back down again.

☺ ☺ ☺ ☺ ☺ ☺ ☺ ☺

The Chelm Tzedakah Box
The shammash of the shul decided to install a poor box so that the fortunate might share their wealth with the poor people. On the eve of the Sabbath, he announced to the congregation that a new opportunity for mitzvot (good deeds) was available. "But," one member complained, "it will be so easy for robbers to steal from the box." The shammash thought long and hard that night, and announced the next day that he had come up with a solution. Pointing upward, he showed, the poor box was now

suspended from a chain at the ceiling, high overhead. "But now how do we put money in the box?"

The next week, the congregation saw the wonderful solution. A lovely circular stairway now ascended to the poor box making it easy to contribute.

☺ ☺ ☺ ☺ ☺ ☺ ☺ ☺

The Rabbi of Chelm

A wise man from Chelm came to the rabbi with this question. "Why is it that if you drop a slice of bread with butter on it that it always lands with the buttered side down?"

"I don't know if that is true," said the rabbi. "Let's try it and see." And so the rabbi buttered a slice of bread and dropped it. But the buttered side was facing up.

"Nu," said the rabbi, "you obviously are working from a false premise."

"But Rabbi," the wise man replied, "you obviously buttered the wrong side."

☺ ☺ ☺ ☺ ☺ ☺ ☺ ☺

A Riddle from Chelm

A Chelm comedian once asked a riddle that nobody could answer: "What's purple, hangs on the wall, and whistles?" No one could solve the riddle, so they asked for the answer.

The jokester said: "A herring."

"A herring?" a man said. "A herring isn't purple."

"Nu," said the comedian. "This herring was painted purple."

"But hanging on a wall? Herrings don't hang on the wall."

"Fooled you. This herring was hung on the wall."

Someone else shouted, "But a herring doesn't whistle."

"All right, so I exaggerated a little."

☺ ☺ ☺ ☺ ☺ ☺ ☺ ☺

Raining in Chelm

Two of the wise men of Chelm were walking down the street when it started to pour.

"Quick, open your umbrella," said one.

"It won't help," his friend said, "my umbrella is full of holes."

"Then why did you bring it?"

"I didn't think it would rain," he said.

☺ ☺ ☺ ☺ ☺ ☺ ☺ ☺

The Railway Station

A visitor once asked one of the wise men of Chelm why they built the railway station three miles from Chelm. The man answered, "We all thought it was a good thing to have it near the trains."

☺ ☺ ☺ ☺ ☺ ☺ ☺ ☺

For the Good of the Economy

In the interests of the economy, saving time and fuel, the Chelm wise men passed a resolution requiring all poultrymen to feed their hens hot water so that they would lay boiled eggs!

☺ ☺ ☺ ☺ ☺ ☺ ☺ ☺

A Chelm Emergency

Chelm was gripped with an emergency. Thieves had entered the town one night and had ransacked several houses. To allay the fears of the townspeople, the rabbi and the council of elders met without delay to ponder what to do with the violators of the law. After long discussion they reached a decision. They issued this declaration to all the citizens of the town:

"Be it known to all Jews of Chelm and to all others who shall enter our town that any thief who shall be apprehended shall be brought without delay to the community hall. Two holes shall be drilled into one of the walls. The thief shall be made to face the wall and place his arms into the holes. On the other side of the wall, he shall be made to tightly grasp a metal rod with his two hands. In this way, we shall prevent him from withdrawing his arms from the holes and escaping.

☺ ☺ ☺ ☺ ☺ ☺ ☺ ☺

The Cemetery Problem

As the generations passed, Chelm's population grew larger. In time, the cemetery was no longer adequate.

Chelm's rabbi summoned the council of elders to devise a plan to solve the problem. For seven days and seven nights they sat together, taking time off only for Shabbat. Many possible solutions were heard and discussed, and each one was carefully examined. At last the elders gave their unanimous support to the proposal that additional land be acquired adjacent to the existing cemetery. They also devised a plan to determine how much land would be needed.

On the next Sabbath a proclamation was read aloud in the synagogue to all Jews in Chelm: "Fellow Chelmites, be advised that tomorrow all Jews of our community, the elderly and not elderly, men, women, and children, without exception, are to gather in the field adjacent to the cemetery. They are to lie down side-by-side, row-by-row. In that way we shall determine precisely how much new burial land we shall need to meet our needs."

☺ ☺ ☺ ☺ ☺ ☺ ☺ ☺

Medical Issue

A group of Chelm's wisest citizens sat engrossed in an important medical issue. "Are the doctors correct when they say that smoking is injurious to health? If they are right, we shall have to take steps to protect the lives of the Jews of Chelm."

One of the group expressed his firm opinion: "The physicians are always trying to frighten us. It is not true that smoking is harmful. My father smoked all his life and he lived to ninety."

A second person agreed: "Smoking has nothing to do with health. I had a baby brother. He never once touched a cigarette, and he died at age two."

☺ ☺ ☺ ☺ ☺ ☺ ☺ ☺

A Herring and a Loaf of Bread

A Chelm housewife went to the market to buy a herring and a loaf of bread. "How much are they," she asked. "Fourteen kopeks," she was told.

"Fourteen kopeks for a herring and bread," she replied. Concerned that the merchant was asking an unfair price, she said: "I think you made a mistake. It should be eleven kopeks."

The merchant replied, "No way. The bread is seven kopeks, and the herring is seven. That comes to fourteen."

The woman persisted and said: "The way I calculate, seven plus seven equal eleven, not fourteen."

The merchant was amazed by her arithmetic, "What kind of strange calculation are you using? Seven and seven are always fourteen."

Again the customer persisted, "Let me show you why it's eleven. I have four children from my first husband. After his death, I married a widower. He, too, had four children from his first marriage. He and I have been blessed with three additional children. That means that I'm the mother of seven children and he is the father of seven children, but between us there are eleven children. Seven and seven are eleven."

☺ ☺ ☺ ☺ ☺ ☺ ☺ ☺

The Songbird

The Jews of Chelm beheld everything in nature as a gift from God. One warm, summer day, two Chelmites reclined in a grassy field, marveling at how the wonders about them testify to the matchless wisdom of the Creator. In a nearby meadow, a cow was munching on the grass, while overhead a songbird was chirping a sweet melody as it flew in lazy circles above the meadow.

One Jew asked the other, "Why is it that the Creator gave wings to the birds, but not to the cows?"

Just as the other Jew opened his mouth to answer, the songbird swooped down low and let fall a splattering that landed on his head. His companion watched him wipe himself clean and said, "Never mind, I think I have just received an answer to my question."

☺ ☺ ☺ ☺ ☺ ☺ ☺ ☺

The Terrible Error in Chelm

It had been a harsh winter in Chelm. As the bitter winter was coming to an end, Chelm's most famous sage was observed sitting alone in his home, silent and brooding. His friends, out of concern for him, tried to find out the source of his sadness. He said to them, "I'm upset because our wise rabbis of old made a terrible error when they arranged our calendar. They ordained that in a Jewish leap year we must have two months of Adar while it is still winter. Had I been among them, I would have protested the terrible harm they have caused to every

Jew in every generation. I would have said to them, 'Honored rabbis, let the doubled month be observed in the summer, in the month of Tammuz, the hottest month of the year, when we don't need boots because of the snow, and when we don't have to chop down trees to heat our homes.'"

☺ ☺ ☺ ☺ ☺ ☺ ☺ ☺

The Sun Versus the Moon

A Jew of Chelm sought out the rabbi for advice on how to solve a problem that had long been vexing him. "Rabbi," he asked, "Which is more important, the sun or the moon?"

The rabbi thought for several minutes, examining the question from every angle.

After much thought, he carefully expressed his opinion, "The moon is more important than the sun. The moon shines at night when we need the light, whereas the sun shines in the daytime when we really don't need it."

☺ ☺ ☺ ☺ ☺ ☺ ☺ ☺

Swimming Logic

A Chelmite sage went bathing in the lake and almost drowned. When he raised an outcry, other swimmers came to his rescue. As he was assisted out of the water, he took a solemn oath: "I swear never to go into the water again until I learn how to swim."

Chapter Seven
A Potpourri of Jewish Humor

This chapter will present an array of jokes on a variety of topics. I hope that you will enjoy, and that they will make you smile.

☺ ☺ ☺ ☺ ☺ ☺ ☺ ☺

New Jewish Dictionary
JEWBILATION: Pride in finding out that one's favorite singer is Jewish.
TORAHFIED: The inability to recall one's lines when called to read from the Torah.
SANTASHMANTA: The explanation given to Jewish kids for why they celebrate Hanukkah while the rest of the world celebrates Christmas.
MATZILATION: Smashing a piece of matzah into small pieces while trying to butter it.
GOYFER: A gentile messenger.
JEWDO: A traditional form of self-defense based on talking one's way out of a tight position.
MEINSTEIN: My son, the genius.
ROSH HASHANAHANA: A rock band from Brooklyn.
MINYASTICS: Going to amazing lengths to find a tenth person to complete the minyan.

☺ ☺ ☺ ☺ ☺ ☺ ☺ ☺

Hebonics

Question: "What time is it?"
English Answer: "Sorry, I don't know."
Hebonic Answer: "What am I, a clock?"

Remark: "I hope things turn out okay."
English Answer: "Thanks."
Hebonic Response: "I should *be* so lucky."

Remark: Hurry up. "Dinner's ready."
English Response: "Be right there."
Hebonic Response: "All right already. I'm coming. What's the hurry? Is there a fire?"

Remark: "I like the tie you gave me. I wear it all the time."
English response: "Glad you like it."
Hebonic answer: "So what's the matter? You don't like the other ties I gave you?"

To guest of honor at his birthday party:
English Response: "Happy Birthday!"
Hebonic remark: "A year smarter you should become."

Answering a phone call from a child:
English remark: "It's been a long time since you called."
Hebonic remark: "You didn't wonder if I'm dead yet?"

☺   ☺   ☺   ☺   ☺   ☺   ☺   ☺

A Potpourri of Jewish Humor

Jewish Jeopardy
We give the answer; you give the question.
A. Midrash.
Q. What is a Middle-Eastern skin disease?
A. The Gaza Strip.
Q. What is an Egyptian belly dance?
A. A classroom, Passover ceremony, and a latke.
Q. What are cheder, seder, and tater?
A. Sofer.
Q. On what do Jews recline?
A. Babylon.
Q. What do rabbis do during their sermons?
A. Filet mignon.
Q. What do you call steaks ordered by 10 Jews?
A. Kishke, sukkah, and circumcision.
Q. What are gut, hut, and cut?

☺ ☺ ☺ ☺ ☺ ☺ ☺ ☺

Feasting and Fasting Laughter
Following is some humorous advice that relates to the Jewish holidays in a nutshell. Enjoy.
Rosh Hashanah—Feast
Tzom Gedalia—Fast
Yom Kippur—More fasting
Sukkot—Feast
Hoshanah Rabbah—More feasting
Simchat Torah—Keep feasting
Month of Heshvan—No feasts or fasts for the entire month
Chanukah—Eat latkes
Tenth of Tevet—Don't eat latkes

Tu B'Shevat—Feast

Fast of Esther—Fast

Purim—Eat pastry

Passover—Don't eat pastry

Shavuot—Dairy feast (blintzes, cheesecake)

Seventeenth of Tammuz—Fast (no blintzes or cheesecake)

Tisha B'Av—Very strict fast (don't let mind even think of cheesecake)

Month of Elul—End of cycle. Enroll in CEDBH (Center for Eating Disorders Before High Holy Days arrive once again)

☺ ☺ ☺ ☺ ☺ ☺ ☺ ☺

Paskin-Rabbis' Ice Cream
Following are the many flavors of this newest glatt kosher ice cream.

Maccabean

Leviticustard

Olive Hashalom

L'chu Vanillcha

Wailing Walnut

Cherry bim cherry bum

Yasher Cocoach

Bubble Gumora

Lemontations

Chocolitvak

Meshuganougat

Soda and Gomorra

Manishta Nut

Rachma Nut

Moishmallow
Chazalnut
Halava-Chomer
Oy Vey Iz
Rashi Road
Balak Berry
Lubavitcher Resberre
Molly Pecan
Cashew Lepesach
Mi Kamocha
Brand Ice
Berry Pri Hagafen
Carmel Shake
ChocEilat Chip

☺   ☺   ☺   ☺   ☺   ☺   ☺   ☺

The Pope and the Synagogue Janitor

One Pope, in the Dark Ages, decreed that all of the Jews had to leave Rome. The Jews did not want to leave, so the Pope challenged them to a disputation to prove that they could remain. No one, however, wanted the responsibility, until finally the shul janitor, Moshe, volunteered. As there was nobody else who wanted to go, Moshe was given the task. But because he knew only Hebrew, a silent debate was agreed.

The day of the debate arrived, and they went to St. Peter's Square to sort out the decision.

First, the Pope waved his hand around his head. Moshe pointed firmly at the ground.

The Pope, in some surprise, held up three fingers. In response, Moshe gave him the middle finger. The crowd started to complain, but the Pope thoughtfully waved them to be quiet. He took out a bottle of wine and a wafer, holding them up. Moshe took out an apple, and held it up. The Pope, to the people's surprise, said, "I concede. This man is too good. The Jews can stay."

Later, the Pope was asked what the debate had meant. He explained, "First I showed him the Heavens, to show that God is everywhere. He pointed at the ground to signify that God is right here with us. I then showed him three fingers, for the Trinity. He reminded me that there is One God common to both our religions. I showed him wine and a wafer, for God's forgiveness. With an apple, he showed me original sin. The man was a master of silent debate."

In the Jewish corner, Moshe had the same question put to him, and answered: "It was all nonsense, really. First, he told me that this whole town would be free of Jews. I told him, Go to Hell. We're staying right here. Then, he told me we had three days to get out. I told him just what I thought of that proposal."

An older woman asked, "But what about the part at the end?" "That" said Moshe with a shrug. "Well, I saw him take out his lunch, so I took out mine."

☺ ☺ ☺ ☺ ☺ ☺ ☺ ☺

An Extremely Wealthy Person

A meshulach comes knocking on a very wealthy person's door, and when the man of the house answers, the meshulach greets him: "Shalom Aleichem, Mr. Goldstein. I'm collecting for the Lotsa Gelt Yeshivah, and I am wondering if a nice wealthy person like yourself would want to make a contribution."

The homeowner answers, "The name is God, not Goldberg, and I'm not Jewish."

"Are you sure?" asks the meshulach.

"Sir, I am positive," replies the homeowner.

"But," says the meshulach," it says here that you're Jewish, and my records are never wrong."

"I can assure you that I am certainly not Jewish," replies the homeowner, getting more and more impatient.

"Look, sir, I know that my records are never wrong. You must be kidding me. Are you sure you are not Jewish?" demands the meshulach.

"For the last time, sir, I am not Jewish, my father is not Jewish, and my grandfather, alov ha-shalom, wasn't Jewish either."

☺ ☺ ☺ ☺ ☺ ☺ ☺ ☺

Talmudic Arguing

Two Talmud students engage in an argument. One says: "What sweetens the coffee is the sugar put in it."

The second says: "That's wrong. What sweetens the coffee is the act of stirring."

"Then," inquires the first one. "Why do you put sugar in the coffee?"

"That's simple," answers the second one, "To know when you have to stop stirring."

☺ ☺ ☺ ☺ ☺ ☺ ☺ ☺

Talmudic Reasoning

A man once asked his rabbi to explain the meaning of talmudic reasoning.

The rabbi replied: "Well, it's not too easy to explain, but I think I can demonstrate it to you and you will get the point. I will ask you a simple question, and you give the answer. Are your ready?"

The man was ready, so the rabbi continued: "Imagine that two men come out of a chimney—one is dirty, the other clean. Which one takes a bath?"
The intrigued listener immediately replied: "That's easy, Rabbi, the dirty one takes the bath."

"Not so," said the rabbi. "The Talmud would explain that when the men came out, the dirty one looked at the clean one and saw a clean face. Meanwhile the clean one looked at the dirty one and saw a dirty face."

A knowing look, complete with broad smile, flashed onto the man's face.
The rabbi continued, "Now tell me which one takes the bath?" The answer was quick and sure. "Now I get it, Rabbi, the clean one takes the bath."

The rabbi looked just a bit unhappy, but he answered patiently, "No. You see, the Talmud would go on to ask: 'How could two men come out of a chimney and one be clean and one be dirty?'"

☺ ☺ ☺ ☺ ☺ ☺ ☺ ☺

The Praying Parrot

Meyer was walking home along Delancey Street one day wishing something wonderful would change his life when he passed a pet store and heard a squawking voice shouting in Yiddish: "Quawwwk . . . vus machst du?" (How are you doing).

Meyer rubbed his eyes and ears. He couldn't believe it. The shop owner sprang out the door and grabbed Meyer by the sleeve, asking him to come and check out the parrot.

Meyer stood in front of an African Grey that cocked his little head and said: "Vus? Ir kent reddin Yiddish?"

Meyer turned excitedly to the storeowner, and placed five hundred dollars down on the counter and carried the parrot in his cage away with him. All night he talked with the parrot in Yiddish. He told the parrot about his life in America, about his family, and the parrot listened intently. Finally, they both went to sleep.

Next morning, Meyer began to put on his tefillin, all the while, saying his prayers. The parrot demanded to know what he was doing, and when Meyer explained, the parrot wanted to do it, too. Meyer went out and handmade a miniature set of tefillin (phylacteries) for his parrot. The parrot wanted to learn and pray, so Meyer taught him how to read Hebrew and taught him every prayer in the prayerbook. In time Meyer came to love and count on the parrot as a friend and a Jew.

On the morning of Rosh Hashanah, Meyer rose, got dressed, and was about to leave when his parrot demanded to go with him. Soon Meyer arrived at shul and brought the parrot in with him. The rabbi and cantor could hardly believe their eyes, and were about to forbid the parrot from entering the sanctuary. However, when Meyer convinced them that his parrot could pray, they allowed the bird inside.

Soon people were making wagers with Meyer regarding his parrot's ability to pray. Thousands of dollars were bet that the parrot could not pray or even speak Yiddish.

All eyes during services were on the parrot. Not a peep, not a word was heard from the parrot. Meyer became very annoyed, and he mumbled under his breath to the bird: "Daven" (Pray).

Nothing, not a single word was uttered.

After Rosh Hashanah services ended, Meyer found that he owed his shul buddy and the rabbi over four thousand dollars. He went home very upset. Finally, several blocks from the shul, the bird, happy as a lark, began to sing an old Yiddish song. Meyer stopped and looked at him. "You miserable bird, you cost me over four thousand dollars. Why? After I made your tefillin, taught you the morning prayers, taught you to read Hebrew. And after you begged me to bring you to synagogue on Rosh Hashanah. Why? Why do this to me now?"

"Don't be a shlemiel!" (fool) the parrot replied. "Think of the odds on Yom Kippur."

☺ ☺ ☺ ☺ ☺ ☺ ☺ ☺

Jewish Beggar

An old Jewish beggar was out on the street in Chicago with his tin cup.

"Please, sir," he pleaded to a passerby, "Could you spare eighty-five cents for a cup of coffee and some pie?"

The man asked, "Where do you get coffee and pie for eighty-five cents in Chicago? It costs at least two dollars."

The beggar replied, "So, who buys retail?"

☺ ☺ ☺ ☺ ☺ ☺ ☺ ☺

Kvetching

A Jewish man in a hospital tells the doctor he wants to be transferred to a different hospital.

The doctor says: "What's wrong? Is it the food?"

"No," the food is fine. I can't kvetch" (complain).

"Is it the room?"

"No, the room is fine. I can't kvetch."

"Is it the staff?"

"No, everyone on the staff is fine. I can't kvetch."

"Then, why do you want to be transferred?"

"I can't kvetch."

☺ ☺ ☺ ☺ ☺ ☺ ☺ ☺

Soviet Union Humor

Q. Rabinovich, what's a fortune?

A. A fortune is to live in our socialist motherland.

Q. And what's a misfortune?

A. A misfortune is to have such a fortune.

☺ ☺ ☺ ☺ ☺ ☺ ☺ ☺

One-Hundredth Birthday

A Jewish man was being interviewed on his one-hundredth birthday. Naturally, he was asked to what he attributed his length of years.

He answered, "I never have smoked, drunk alcohol, or overeaten. I go to bed early and get up early."

"You know," said the reporter, "I had an uncle who lived exactly that way, and he only lived to the age of ninety. To what do you attribute that?"

The Jewish man replied: "He just didn't keep it up long enough!"

☺ ☺ ☺ ☺ ☺ ☺ ☺ ☺

The Hebrew Blessing

An eight-year-old nephew visited us during his summer vacation. At the evening meal, I invited him to lead us in the Hebrew blessing over the bread. He protested that he had forgotten it.

"Forgot it?" I exclaimed in mock surprise. "Why, you just learned it in Hebrew school."

"Uncle Sidney," he explained with a twinkle, "I have a very good forgettory."

☺ ☺ ☺ ☺ ☺ ☺ ☺ ☺

One Good Deed

A man tries to enter heaven but is stopped by the angel who keeps the Pearly Gates. The angel explains that it is not easy to get into heaven. There is a certain criterion to be met before entry is allowed.

The angel asks the man several questions.

Was he religious in life?

He answers no.

Did he attend shul on Shabbat and Holy Days?

He answers no.

Did he give tzedakah (charity) to the poor?

130

He answers again no.
Did he do any good deeds while on earth?
He answers no.
Did he help his neighbor?
He answers no.
The angel says: "Not good, not good at all." In exasperation the angel says, "Look, everybody does something nice sometime. Work with me, I'm trying to help. Now think."

The man says, "There was this little old lady who was surrounded by a dozen Hell's Angels when I came out of the drugstore. They had taken her purse and were shoving her, taunting her, and abusing her. I got so mad, I threw my bags down, fought my way through the crowd, and got her purse back. I helped her to her feet. Then I went up to the biggest, meanest biker and told him how despicable, cowardly, and mean he was. And then I spit in his face."

"Wow," says the angel, "that's impressive. When did this happen?"

"Oh, about ten minutes ago," replied the man.

☺ ☺ ☺ ☺ ☺ ☺ ☺ ☺

The Jewish Genie
Jacob was walking on the beach and noticed an old lamp. He picked it up and rubbed it. A genie suddenly came out of the bottle and said, "Thanks Jacob. I've been locked up in this bottle for over two hundred years. Just for that I'll grant you three wishes. However, I warn you that what you get, your lawyer will get double."

Jacob thought for a while and said, "For my first wish I'd like one hundred million gold coins."

The genie said: "Okay, but remember, your lawyer will get two hundred million gold coins."

Jacob said: "That's fine with me."

Then the genie granted Jacob's wish. Poof. There right in front of him was a hundred million coins.

Then Jacob said, "For my second wish I would like a fifty-acre ranch on the French Riviera with a thirty-room home overlooking the ocean bluffs.

The genie said, "Okay, but remember, your lawyer will be next door with twice the acreage and in a house twice as large, and he likes to party twenty-four hours a day."

Jacob said: "I think I can live with that."

Then the genie granted Jacob's wish. Poof. Right there he was, on the French Riviera and next door was his attorney just as the genie had said.

So the genie said, "For your third wish you'd better think long and hard."

So after thinking it over, Jacob said, "Could you please scare me half to death?"

☺ ☺ ☺ ☺ ☺ ☺ ☺ ☺

Jewish Tricks

Mr. Henry, the math teacher, walked into the classroom, and three students were fooling around and not in their seats. Very disturbed, Mr. Henry, the math teacher, decided to teach them a lesson.

"Ivan, give me a two-digit number."

"Sixty-five," he replied.

"Why not fifty-six? For this you get a D."
"Walter, give me a two-digit number."
He answered: "Ninety-four."
"Why not forty-nine?" For this you get a D."
"Sammy, give me a two-digit number.
"Thirty-three."
"Alright, Sammy, stop with the Jewish tricks."

☺ ☺ ☺ ☺ ☺ ☺ ☺ ☺

The Execution

Three men, a Frenchman, an Italian, and a Jew were condemned to be executed. Their captor told them they had the right to have a last meal of their choice before execution. The Frenchman ordered some good French wine and a French bread. He ate it and was executed.

The Italian ordered a large plate of pasta. He ate it and was executed.

The Jewish fellow asked for a large bowl of strawberries. The captor said: "We're now in September; strawberries are not in season and won't be for months."

To this the Jewish fellow replied: "I'll wait."

☺ ☺ ☺ ☺ ☺ ☺ ☺ ☺

A Jew and a Chinaman

A Jewish man and a Chinese man were conversing. The Jewish man commented upon what a wise people the Chinese are.

"Yes," replied the Chinese man. "Our culture is over four thousand years old. But you Jews are a very wise people, too."

The Jewish man responded, "Yes, our culture is over five thousand years old."

The Chinese man was incredulous. "That's impossible," he replied. "Where did you people eat for a thousand years?"

☺ ☺ ☺ ☺ ☺ ☺ ☺ ☺

Buzz Off

One day, two bees are buzzing around what's left of a rose bush.

"How's your summer been?" asks bee number one.

"Not too good," says bee two. "Lots of rain, lots of cold. There aren't enough flowers, therefore not enough pollen."

The first bee has an idea. "Hey, why don't you go down to the corner and hang a left. There's a bar mitzvah going on. Plenty of flowers and fruit."

Bee two buzzes, "Thanks," and takes off. One hour later, the bees bump into each other again.

"How was the bar mitzvah?" asks the first bee.

"Great," replies the second.

The first bee, however, notices a small circle on his friend's head, and inquires, "What's that on your head?"

"A yarmulke," is the answer. "I didn't want them to think I was a wasp."

☺ ☺ ☺ ☺ ☺ ☺ ☺ ☺

Components of the Dell Shalom Computer
Following are the attributes of the newest in a line of kosher computers by Dell, called the Dell Shalom:

Instead of getting a General Protection Fault error, the PC now gets Ferklempt (misguided);

The PC shuts down automatically at sundown on Friday evening;

After the computer dies, one must dispose of it within twenty-four hours;

The multimedia player has been renamed to "Nu, so play my music already";

I hear "Hava Nagila" during startup;

Microsoft Office includes, "A little byte of this, a little byte of that";

When my PC works too hard, I hear a loud "Oy, gevalt" (OMG);

Computer viruses can now be cured with matzah-ball chicken soup;

When the spell-check finds an error, it prompts: "Is this the best you can do?"

If you have this kosher computer, you can't get spam.

☺   ☺   ☺   ☺   ☺   ☺   ☺   ☺

Stranded in the Wilderness
A Russian, a Frenchman, and a Jew are stranded in the wilderness. After trudging along for miles, the Russian exclaims: "I'm tired. I'm thirsty. I must have vodka."

A few minutes pass, and next the Frenchman cries: "I'm tired. I'm thirsty. I must have wine."

135

The group walks a little further and finally the Jew shouts: "I'm tired. I'm thirsty. I must have diabetes."

☺ ☺ ☺ ☺ ☺ ☺ ☺ ☺

Bubbe's Driving

Sitting on the side of the highway waiting to catch speeding drivers, a state police officer sees a car sputtering along at twenty-two miles per hour. He thinks to himself, "This driver is just as dangerous as a speeder." So he turns on his lights and pulls the driver over.

Approaching the car, he notices that there are five elderly ladies, eyes wide and white as ghosts. Bubbe, obviously confused, says to him, "Officer, I don't understand. I was doing exactly the speed limit. So what's the problem?"

"Ma'am, the officer responds, "you weren't speeding, but you should know that driving slower than the speed limit can also be dangerous to other drivers."

"Slower than the speed limit" she asked. "No sir, I was doing the speed limit—exactly twenty-two miles an hour," Bubbe says proudly.

The state police officer, trying to contain a chuckle, explains to her that 22 was the route number, not the speed limit. A little embarrassed, she grinned and thanked the officer for pointing out the error.

The officer said, "But, before I go ma'am. I have to ask. Is everyone in this car okay? These women seem awfully shaken, and they haven't muttered a single peep this whole time," the officer asks.

Bubbe replied, "Oh, they'll be all right in a minute officer. We just got off Route 119."

☺   ☺   ☺   ☺   ☺   ☺   ☺   ☺

The One-Dollar Bill
A one-dollar bill met his old friend, the twenty-dollar bill, and said, "Hey, where've you been? I haven't seen you around here much."

The twenty answered, "I've been hanging out at the casinos, went on a cruise, and did the rounds of the ship, back to the United States for awhile, went to a couple of baseball games, to the mall, that kind of stuff. How about you?"

The one-dollar bill said, "You know, same old stuff, contribution to shul, pushke, contribution to church, contribution to Fifteenth Street beggar, pushke."

☺   ☺   ☺   ☺   ☺   ☺   ☺   ☺

On the Plane
Rachel did a lot of traveling for her business, so she flew very often. Flying made her very, very nervous, so she always took her prayerbook along so she could read the traveler's prayer. It helped her relax.

One time, she was sitting next to a skeptical man. When he saw her pull out her prayerbook, he gave a chuckle and smirk and went back to what he was doing. After a while, he turned to her and asked, "You don't really believe all that stuff in there?"

Rachel replied, "Of course."

He said, "Well, what about that guy that was swallowed by that whale?"

"Oh, Jonah," responded Rachel.

"Yes, how do you suppose he survived all that time in the whale?"

"Well, I don't really know. I guess when I get to heaven, I will ask him."

"What if he isn't there?" the man asked sarcastically.

"Then you can ask him," replied Rachel.

☺ ☺ ☺ ☺ ☺ ☺ ☺ ☺

Jewish and Christian Kids
Jewish Child: "Our rebbe wears this fur hat."
Catholic Child: "So? our priest wears a collar."
Jewish Child: "What's so special about a collar?"
Catholic Child: "You know, kills ticks and fleas up to six months."

☺ ☺ ☺ ☺ ☺ ☺ ☺ ☺

The Brother-in-Law
Mr. Stein was brought to the hospital and taken quickly in for coronary surgery. The operation went well and as the groggy man regained consciousness, he was reassured by the doctor, who was waiting by his bed.

"You're going to be just fine, Mr. Stein," the doctor said.

The doctor was joined by a nurse, who said, "We do need to know, however, how you intend to pay for your stay here. Are you covered by insurance?"

Mr. Stein responded, "No, I'm not."

"Then, can you pay in cash?" the nurse persisted.

"I'm afraid I can't."

"Well, do you have any close relatives?" the nurse questioned sternly.

"Just my sister in New York," he said. "But she converted to . . . she's a nun . . . in fact, a real spinster."

"Oh, I must correct you, Mr. Stein. Nuns are not spinsters; they are married to God."

"Wonderful, wonderful," Mr. Stein said. "In that case, please send my bill to my brother-in-law."

☺ ☺ ☺ ☺ ☺ ☺ ☺ ☺

A Canine Riddle

Q. What's the difference between a Jewish mother-in-law and a Rottweiler?

A. Eventually the Rottweiler lets go.

☺ ☺ ☺ ☺ ☺ ☺ ☺ ☺

Three Wishes

A secretary, a paralegal, and a partner in a city Jewish law firm are walking through a park on their way to lunch when they find an antique oil lamp. They rub it and a genie comes out in a puff of smoke.

The genie says: "I usually only grant three wishes, so I'll give each of you just one."

"Me first. Me first." says the secretary. "I want to be in the Bahamas, driving a speedboat, without a care in the world." Poof. She's gone.

In astonishment, "Me next. Me next," says the parale-gal. "I want to be in Hawaii, relaxing on the beach with my personal masseuse, an endless supply of piña coladas, and the love of my life." Poof. She's gone.

"You're next," the genie says to the partner. The part-ner says, " I want those two back in the office immedi-ately after lunch."

☺ ☺ ☺ ☺ ☺ ☺ ☺ ☺

Loyalty
Morris is being indoctrinated by the Russian government.

Government Official: "If you had a yacht, what would you do with it?"

Morris: "Give it to Mother Russia."

Government Official: And if you had a palace, what would you do with it?"

Morris: "Give it to Mother Russia."

Government Official: "And if you had a sweater, what would you do with it?"

No reply.

Government official asks the question again.

Still no reply.

Finally, he shouts: "Morris, why don't you reply?"

Morris: "Because I have a sweater."

☺ ☺ ☺ ☺ ☺ ☺ ☺ ☺

The Obituary
A Jewish lady calls the newspaper and asks for the obitu-ary. The obit guy asks: "What can I do for you?"

"I'd like to place an obituary."

"All right, how would you like it to read?"

"'Irving Levine died.'"

"That's it? 'Irving Levine died'?"

"That's it."

"But you get four lines in the obit. It's included in the price."

"All right. 'Irving Levine died. . . . Cadillac for sale.'"

☺ ☺ ☺ ☺ ☺ ☺ ☺ ☺

Florida Vacation

A New York Jewish man left the snowy city for a vacation in Florida. His wife was on a business trip in Atlanta and was planning to join him in Florida the next day. When Jacob reached his hotel, he decided to send his wife a quick e-mail.

Unable to find the scrap of paper on which he had written her e-mail address, he did his best to type it from memory. Unfortunately, he missed one letter, and his note was directed instead to an elderly rebbitzin (rabbi's wife) whose husband had passed away only the day before. When the grieving rebbetzin checked her e-mail, she took one look at the monitor, let out a piercing scream, and fell to the floor dead. At the sound, her family rushed into the room and saw this note on the screen:

> Dearest Wife,
> Just got checked in. Everything prepared for your arrival tomorrow.
> Your loving husband
> PS Sure is hot down here.

☺ ☺ ☺ ☺ ☺ ☺ ☺ ☺

Tale of the Sultan

One morning during prayer services a loud boom and a sudden flash of smoke appeared in the front of our congregation. When the smoke cleared, the astonished congregation saw this frightening figure in red complete with horns, pitchfork, a tail, and a ~~yarmulke.~~

Immediately the congregation panicked. People rushed to the back ~~of the shul~~ trying to get away. The Devil watched the retreat with great glee, but his mood was disturbed by the sight of one man still relaxing comfortably in the third row right side in his pew.

Angrily, the Devil thundered: "Do you know who I am?"

Jacob replied in a nonchalant way, "Sure I do."

The Devil was extremely puzzled. "Do you not fear me?"

"Nope. Not at all," came the reply.

Jacob snorted, "What for? I've been married to your sister for thirty five years!"

FV.
1.22. 10

☺ ☺ ☺ ☺ ☺ ☺ ☺ ☺

The Genius Riddle

Q. What's a genius?
A. An average student with a Jewish mother.

☺ ☺ ☺ ☺ ☺ ☺ ☺ ☺

Shipwrecked

A Jewish sailor was shipwrecked on a desert island and the first thing he did was build two synagogues. Years later, when he was rescued, people were bewildered and asked him why he built two synagogues.

He replied: "Oh, that other one. I would never go there."

☺ ☺ ☺ ☺ ☺ ☺ ☺ ☺

Jewish Riddles

Q. What did the waiter ask the group of dining Jewish mothers?
A. Is anything all right?
Q. What do Jewish wives make for supper?
A. Reservations.

I.O.U.

Ginsberg never pays his bills and is seen bargaining with a supplier. "Hey Ginsberg," Goldberg asks him, "why are you knocking that man's prices down. You're never going to pay him anyway."

"Listen," answers Ginsberg, "he's a nice chap. I just want to keep down his losses!"

☺ ☺ ☺ ☺ ☺ ☺ ☺ ☺

Going for a Drive

Ben was driving down the road and gets pulled over by a cop. Walking up to Ben's car, the cop says: "Your wife fell out of the car five miles back."

Ben replies, "Thank God for that. I'd thought I'd gone deaf."

☺ ☺ ☺ ☺ ☺ ☺ ☺ ☺

Jewish Lawyer

Velvel was critically ill. Feeling that death was near, he called his lawyer.

"I want to become a lawyer. How much is it for that express degree you told me about?"

"It's $50,000," the lawyer said. "But why? You'll be dead soon, so why do you want to become a lawyer?"

"That's my business," answers Velvel. "Get me the course."

Four days later, Velvel got his law degree. His lawyer was at his bedside making sure his bill would be paid.

Suddenly, the old man was racked with fits of coughing, and it was clear that this would be the end. Still curious, the lawyer leaned over and said, "Please Velvel, before it's too late, tell me why you wanted to get a law degree so badly before you died?"

In a faint whisper, as he breathed his last breath, Velvel said: "One less Jewish lawyer."

☺ ☺ ☺ ☺ ☺ ☺ ☺ ☺

The Loan

"Hello."

"Hello—that's you, Abe?"

"Yes, dis is Abe."

"It doesn't sound like Abe."

"Vell, dis is Abe all right."

"You're positive, it's Abe."

"Absolutely."

"Vell, listen Abie, dis is Moe. Can you lend me feefty dolluhs?"

"Ven Abe comes in, I'll tell him you called."

☺ ☺ ☺ ☺ ☺ ☺ ☺ ☺

The Shadchan Quip

The Jewish boy and girl went on a stroll. The boy said to the shadchan (Jewish matchmaker) when next they met: "She limps."

"Only when she walks," agreed the shadchan.

☺ ☺ ☺ ☺ ☺ ☺ ☺ ☺

Noodle Soup

A man went into a kosher restaurant in New York and ordered a full course dinner. He started off his meal with soup. After the first spoonful he made a sour face.

"Waiter," he called out. This cabbage soup isn't sour enough."

"Who told you it was cabbage soup," said the waiter. "This is noodle soup, mister."

"Oh, so it's noodles," sighed the customer. "Well, for noodle soup it's sour enough."

☺ ☺ ☺ ☺ ☺ ☺ ☺ ☺

The Self-Admiring Chazzan

A certain cantor greatly admired his own singing voice. It was but one example of his lack of humility. At the end of the Rosh Hashanah service, he sought a compliment from the president of the congregation.

"What did you think of my singing today?"

The president, well aware of the chazzan's limitless vanity, replied, "I was dazzled by your amazing memory."

Puzzled by the president's words, he asked, "What has my memory got to do with my singing?"

The president responded: "You made the identical mistakes this year that you made last year."

☺ ☺ ☺ ☺ ☺ ☺ ☺ ☺

The Jewish Saloonkeeper

A Jewish saloonkeeper, proud but ignorant, was determined to raise his son with Jewish knowledge. He hired a learned tutor to teach the child Hebrew. The boy, as it happened, was quite slow-witted. One day the father saw the tutor laboriously repeating the words of the Mourner's Kaddish with the child. He became indignant and accosted the tutor, "How dare you teach my son a prayer to mourn my death?"

The tutor responded, "Don't worry. You'll be a very old man by the time your son masters the words of the Kaddish."

☺ ☺ ☺ ☺ ☺ ☺ ☺ ☺

146

The Shtetl Jew

A shtetl Jew arrived in the big city on a Friday. It was his first experience away from his hometown. The next morning he set out on foot to attend Shabbat prayers. On his way to the synagogue, he passed a number of Jewish merchants who sat in front of their open shops waiting for customers to arrive. For them, the Shabbat was no different from any other day of the week.

Shocked and confused by what he saw, he continued on his way. A storekeeper saw him and called out, "Come in. All men's suits are available at seventy percent off."

Greatly upset by this desecration of the Sabbath, the visitor shouted back: "Shame on you. Isn't it enough that you are violating the Sabbath? Must you also announce it for the whole world to hear?"

The storekeeper shot back, "I'm forced to sell good-quality suits at seventy percent off, and you call that doing business on Shabbat?"

☺ ☺ ☺ ☺ ☺ ☺ ☺ ☺

Beggar Jew

A beggar Jew wandered from village to village searching for a person who would take pity on him. He stumbled into a village where he was overcome by the delicious aroma of freshly cooked food coming from an open window. He knocked at the door, hoping for a bite to eat. A woman opened the door and demanded to know what he wished.

"Please," he said. "I'm a poor man. I haven't had a decent meal for days. I beg you to please help me." She replied, "Would you eat some cold soup."

Eagerly, he answered, "Yes."

"In that case," she said, "come back tomorrow. The soup is still hot."

☺ ☺ ☺ ☺ ☺ ☺ ☺ ☺

Signs on Synagogue Bulletin Board

Under same management for over 5769 years.

Don't give up. Moses was once a basket case.

What part of "Thou shall not" don't you understand?

Shul committees should be made up of three members, two of whom should be absent every meeting.

Any time a person goes into a deli and orders pastrami on white bread, somewhere a Jew dies.

☺ ☺ ☺ ☺ ☺ ☺ ☺ ☺

The Mezuzahs

A wealthy Jewish man buys a fabulous home in Beverly Hills, California. He brings in a local workman to decorate the place. When the job is finished, the homeowner is delighted but realizes that he's forgotten to put mezuzahs (receptacles with sacred parchment) on the doors. He goes out and buys fifty mezuzahs and asks the decorator to place them on the right-hand side of each door except bathrooms and kitchen. He's really worried that the decorator will chip the paint or won't put them

148

up correctly. However, when he comes back a few hours later, he sees that the job has been carried out to his entire satisfaction. He's so pleased that he gives the decorator a bonus.

As the decorator is walking out of the door he says, "Glad you're happy with the job. By the way, I took out all the warranties in the little boxes and left them on the table for you."

☺ ☺ ☺ ☺ ☺ ☺ ☺ ☺

The Restaurant Switch

A customer in a Jewish restaurant gave his order to the waiter.

"I want some roast duck."

"I'm sorry, we have no roast duck today—only roast goose."
"Ask the boss."

The waiter went to the boss. "Mr. Katz wants roast duck."

"Tell him we have no roast duck today—only roast goose."

"I told him so, but he insists on having roast duck."

The boss sighed and said, "All right, if Katz insists, he insists. Ask the cook to cut off a portion of roast duck from the roast goose."

☺ ☺ ☺ ☺ ☺ ☺ ☺ ☺

Two Old Men

Two old men sat silently over their glasses of tea for what might have been, or at any rate seemed, hours. At last, one spoke: "Oy, veh!"

The other said: "You're telling me."

☺ ☺ ☺ ☺ ☺ ☺ ☺ ☺

High Holy Day Ticket

Mr. Singer went to his synagogue on the High Holy Days to deliver an emergency message to a member praying inside. He was told that he could not go into the shul without a ticket.

Mr. Singer explained that it was an emergency, and all that he wanted to do was to go in and deliver a message to Mrs. Singer.

To which the usher replied: "Okay, but remember, no praying!"

☺ ☺ ☺ ☺ ☺ ☺ ☺ ☺

The Day of Atonement

Morey Adelman was visiting the Fifth Avenue Bakery on Yom Kippur at three in the afternoon. The bakery was abuzz with baskets, carts, and people. Morey approached the cashier and spoke to the man in front of him.
"I thought the bakery wouldn't be so crowded at this time because of the Jewish holiday," Morey said to the man.

The man responded: "Me, too. I thought Jewish people were supposed to be praying in Temple until nightfall.

Nearby a woman pushing a cart laden with baked goodies said: "It's already nightfall in Jerusalem."

☺ ☺ ☺ ☺ ☺ ☺ ☺ ☺

Six Passover Riddles

Q. Why do we have a Haggadah at Passover?

A. So we can seder correct words.

Q. What do you call someone who derives pleasure from the bread of affliction?

A. A matzochist.

Q. What do you get when you eat charoset with chopped liver?

A. Charoses of the liver.

Q. Why did Pharaoh refuse to release the Jews after the first nine plagues?

A. Pharaoh was still in denial.

Q. Why do we say Yizkor on the last day of Passover?

A. On Passover, we remember the Exodus. After Yizkor, there is also a mass exodus in many shuls.

Q. How did Passover get its name?

A. Since people can't often reach the matzah at the Seder table, they often say, "Could you please pass over the matzah?"

☺ ☺ ☺ ☺ ☺ ☺ ☺ ☺

Winter of 1994

The winter of 1994 was a difficult one for European root crops. A week before Passover, the Madrid community found that the shipment of horseradish that it had ordered from Bolivia would not arrive until ten days after the Passover holiday.

The community needed the horseradish for its traditional Passover seder, but each time the Madrid rabbi called the food suppliers, he got the same response: It is not possible to get the horseradish for two weeks.

Finally, the rabbi called a friend of his in Israel, who happened to be a second cousin of the rabbinic kosher food supervisor, and begged him to organize the sending of a crate of horseradish roots by air express to Madrid.

After two days, and only one day before the Festival of Passover, a crate of Israeli horseradish roots was loaded onto an El Al plane in Tel Aviv that was on its way to Madrid. All now seemed well.

Unfortunately, when the rabbi came to the Madrid Airport to take the crate out of customs, he was informed that an unforeseen wildcat strike had just broken out and that no shipments would be unloaded for at least four days.

So, you see, the chreyn (horseradish) in Spain stayed mainly on the plane.

☺ ☺ ☺ ☺ ☺ ☺ ☺ ☺

The Israelites' Complaints

As Moses and the Israelites were crossing the Red Sea, the Israelites began to complain to Moses of how thirsty they were after walking so far. Unfortunately, they were not able to drink from the walls of water on either side of them, as they were made up of salt water.

Then, a fish from that wall of water told Moses that he and his family heard the complaints of the people, but that they, through their own gills, could remove the salt from the water and force it out of their mouths like a fresh water fountain for the Israelites to drink as they walked by.

Moses accepted this kindly fish's offer. But before the fish and his family began to help, they told Moses they had a demand. They and their descendants had to be always present at the seder meal that would be established to commemorate the Exodus, since they had a part in the story. When Moses agreed to this, he gave them their name, which remains how they are known to this very day, for he said to them, "Go filter, fish."

☺ ☺ ☺ ☺ ☺ ☺ ☺ ☺

Arguing in Shul

A young scholar from New York was invited to become rabbi in a small community in Chicago. On his very first Sabbath, a hot debate erupted as to whether one should or should not stand during the reading of the Ten Commandments.

Next day, the rabbi visited ninety-eight-year-old Mr. Katz in the nursing home. "Mr. Katz, I'm asking you as the oldest member of the community," said the rabbi, "what is our synagogue's custom during the reading of the Ten Commandments?

"Why do you ask?" retorted Mr. Katz.

"Yesterday we read the Ten Commandments. Some people stood, some people sat. The ones standing started screaming at the ones seated, telling them to stand up. The ones sitting started screaming at the ones standing, telling them to sit down."

"That," said the old man, "is our custom."

☺ ☺ ☺ ☺ ☺ ☺ ☺ ☺

Two Grandmothers

Two very Jewish bubbes were enjoying the sunshine on a park bench in New York. They had been meeting at the same park every sunny day for over fifteen years, chatting and enjoying the company of each other.

One day, the younger of the two ladies turned to the other and said, "Please don't be angry with me, dear, but I am embarrassed, after all these years. What is your name? I'm trying to remember, but I just can't."

The older friend stared at her, looked very distressed, and said nothing for two full minutes, and finally with tearful eyes, "How soon do you have to know?"

☺ ☺ ☺ ☺ ☺ ☺ ☺ ☺

Going Up to the Torah

A gabbai approaches a guest in the synagogue and says, "I want to give you an aliyah (Torah honor). What's your name?"

The man says, "Sarah bat Moshe" (Sarah the daughter of Moses).

The gabbai says, "No, I need *your* name."

The man repeats, "Sarah bat Moshe."

The Gabbai asks, "How can that be your name?"

The man replies: "I've been having big financial problems, so everything is in my wife's name."

☺ ☺ ☺ ☺ ☺ ☺ ☺ ☺

A Post Office Joke

A man went to the post office to buy stamps for her Chanukah cards.

"What denomination?" asked the clerk.

"Oh, good heavens. Have we come to this?" replied the woman. "Give me fifty Conservative, two Orthodox, and thirty-seven Reform."

☺ ☺ ☺ ☺ ☺ ☺ ☺ ☺

Jewish Witness

Mr. Katz is called as a witness in a trial.

"How old are you?" asks the D.A.

"I am, *keyneynhoroh* (may the evil eye not strike me), ninety-one."

"Excuse me," what did you say?"

"I said, I am, *keyneynhoroh*, ninety-one years old."

"Sir, the clerk can't type unusual words. Please just answer the question with no embellishments," says the D.A. "I ask you again, how old are you?"

"I told you: *Keyneynhoroh*, I'm ninety-one."

The D.A. is now getting superannoyed. The judge, too, is beginning to lose patience. He instructs: "The witness will answer the question simply and plainly, or be held in contempt of court."

The defense lawyer rises and says, "Your Honor, I think I can resolve this. May I ask the question?"

"If you can get this trial moving along, then be my guest."

"Mr. Katz, let me ask you, *keyneynhoroh*, how old are you?"

Mr. Katz replies, "Ninety-one."

☺ ☺ ☺ ☺ ☺ ☺ ☺ ☺

Typical Bubbe

A Jewish grandma is giving directions to her grown grandson, who is coming to visit his wife: "You come to the front door of the apartment complex. I am in Apt. 15B. There is a big panel on the front door. With your elbow, push 15B. I will then buzz you in.

"Come inside; the elevator is on the right. Get in, and with your elbow, hit 15. When you get out, I am on the left. With your elbow, hit my doorbell."

"Grandma, that sounds easy, but why am I hitting all these buttons with my elbow?"

"What! You're coming empty-handed?"

☺ ☺ ☺ ☺ ☺ ☺ ☺ ☺

F.V. 2-11-10
F.V. 10-18-12

Gefilte Fish Pun

Teacher: Use the word *officiate* in a sentence.
Manny: A Jew got sick from the gefilte officiate.

☺ ☺ ☺ ☺ ☺ ☺ ☺ ☺

The Grief-Stricken Jester

The Jewish jester was grief-stricken and totally overcome with melancholy sickness. His world was soon to come to an end. For a long time he had served the Baghdadian caliph at his court, keeping them amused whenever they called upon him. But he did an unthinkable act, which so much displeased his ruler that he was sentenced to death.

"However," said the caliph, "in consideration of the merriment and jests that you have told me all these many years, I will let you choose how you are to die."

To which the jester responded: "If it is all right with you, I choose death by old age.

☺ ☺ ☺ ☺ ☺ ☺ ☺ ☺

Aren't You Moses?

George W. Bush, in an airport lobby, noticed a man in a long, flowing white robe with a flowing white beard and long white hair. The man had a staff in one hand and some stone tablets under the other arm.

George W. approached the man and asked: "Aren't you Moses?"

The man ignored George W. and stared at the ceiling.

George W. positioned himself more directly in the man's view and asked again, "Aren't you Moses?"

George W. tugged at the man's sleeve and asked him again, "Aren't you Moses?"

The man finally responded in an irritated voice: "Yes, I am."

George W. asked him why he was so uppity and the man answered, "The last time I spoke to a bush, I had to spend forty years in the desert."

☺ ☺ ☺ ☺ ☺ ☺ ☺ ☺

Passover Promos

Here are the top ten failed Passover promotions:

10. U.S. Army "The Army of Who Knows One?"

9. Animal Awareness Passover Campaign "Frogs are our friends, not a plague."

157

8. American Red Cross "This Passover, let's make rivers of blood."

7. Lenox Hill OBGYN "We won't throw your newborn into the Nile."

6. Adoption Promotion Week "Drop your unwanted children in a basket in the NYC Reservoir."

5. D'Angelo's Barber Shop " Free lice check with every haircut."

4. Republic of China's Population Control Agency "Death of the firstborn commemorative pins."

3. eBay "Your afikoman is worth a lot more than that."

2. RadioShack "You've got four questions. We've got answers."

1. Kosher for Passover Ex-Lax "Now in new matzah strength—Ex-odus"

☺   ☺   ☺   ☺   ☺   ☺   ☺   ☺

The Latke Dilemma

It was soon to be Chanukah and the village in Poland was afraid of not having latkes (potato pancakes) because they were entirely out of flour. The villagers called in Rudi the Rabbi to help solve the problem. He said: "Don't worry. I have an idea. Let's substitute matzah meal for flour, and the latkes will still turn out to be great."

Ruthie looked at her husband Morris, and said: "Do you think it will work?"

Morey answered: "Of course, Rudolph the Rab knows grain, dear!"

☺   ☺   ☺   ☺   ☺   ☺   ☺   ☺

Top Five Reasons to Love Chanukah
1. No roof damage from reindeer.
2. Never a silent night when you're among your Jewish loved ones.
3. If someone messes up on their gift, there are still even more days to correct it.
4. Betting Chanukah gelt (money) on candle races.
5. You can use your fireplace.

☺ ☺ ☺ ☺ ☺ ☺ ☺ ☺

Jewish Quotes
"I once wanted to become an atheist, but I gave up. They have no holidays." —Henny Youngman

"Most Texans think Chanukah is some sort of duck call." —Richard Lewis

"My father never lived to see his dream come true of an all-Yiddish-speaking Canada." —David Steinberg

"Look at Jewish history. Unrelieved lamenting would be intolerable. So, for every ten Jews beating their breasts, God designated one to be crazy and amuse the breast-beaters. By the time I was five, I knew that I was that one." —Mel Brooks

"The time is at hand when the wearing of a prayer shawl and skullcap will not bar a man from the White House, unless of course, the man is Jewish." —Jules Farber

"God, I know we are your chosen people, but couldn't you choose somebody else for a change?" —Shalom Aleichem

"Let me tell you the one thing I have against Moses. He took us forty years into the desert in order to bring us to one place in the Middle East that has no oil." —Golda Meir

"Even a secret agent can't lie to a Jewish mother." — Peter Malkin

☺ ☺ ☺ ☺ ☺ ☺ ☺ ☺

Things I Knew Wouldn't Be Taught in Hebrew School
1. The High Holy Days having nothing to do with marijuana.
2. Where there's smoke, there may be salmon.
3. No meal is complete without leftovers.
4. A shmata is a dress that your husband's ex is wearing.
5. After the destruction of the Second Temple, God created Loehmann's.
6. Never take a front row at a bris (circumcision).
7. Next year in Jerusalem. The year after that, how about a nice cruise?
8. Never leave a restaurant empty-handed.
9. Spring ahead, fall back, winter in Boca.
10. The important Jewish holidays are the one on which alternate-side-of-the-street parking is suspended.

☺ ☺ ☺ ☺ ☺ ☺ ☺ ☺

New Jewish Reality TV Shows
Channel 20, WBRW, "TV for your inner Jew" has announced its new season's lineup of reality shows. They include:

"Joe Minyanaire." A good-looking man goes to an Orthodox singles event and tells girls he meets there that he prays every day. Watch their reaction when they find out that he hasn't been inside a synagogue since his bar mitzvah and spends every morning and evening in Dunkin' Donuts.

"American Sheitel." Viewers vote for the woman wearing the best-looking head-covering.

"Schmeer Factor." Contestants view to see who is the bravest by trying new bagel and cream cheese combinations.

"Jewish Survivor." Participants attend a round of Jewish organizational fundraising dinners. Each week, one person is voted off for falling asleep during the guest speaker, complaining about overcooked chicken, eating three extra deserts, or snapping his/her fingers at the rabbi, who looks just like one of the waiters. The final "survivor" wins one million dollars to be donated to his favorite charity.

☺ ☺ ☺ ☺ ☺ ☺ ☺ ☺

If the Entire Space Shuttle Crew Were Israelis
IMAGINE IF, INSTEAD OF ONE ASTRONAUT, THE ENTIRE SPACE SHUTTLE CREW WERE ISRAELIS:

The flight would leave an hour late.

Instead of counting down from ten to blastoff, they'd read *Tefillas ha-Derech* (Prayer for the Journey).

As the astronauts prepared to board the spacecraft, a young girl would ask them who had packed their luggage. She'd write their replies on her hand and nobody would understand why.

At least one of the astronauts would actually be plain-clothes security.

Each astronaut would have his or her own cellphone and spend most of the flight talking while they worked.

After two days in space, the Palestinian Authority would complain to the United Nations and CNN that the Space Shuttle was actually their property and had been for hundreds of years. The next day the U.N. would pass a resolution confirming this.

The Shuttle would take two years for preparation—six months training and a year and a half to argue who gets the seats.

☺ ☺ ☺ ☺ ☺ ☺ ☺ ☺

A Plate of Borsht

Yankel the wagoner was eating a plate of borsht (beet soup) when his neighbor yelled into his kitchen: "Yankel, something horrible has happened."

Yankel continued to eat without interruption.

"Yankel, prepare yourself for really terrible news. Something terrible has happened."

Still Yankel remained unperturbed.

"Yankel, you poor man, your wife has just died."

The news had no apparent effect.

"How can you sit there eating so calmly?" his neighbor inquired. "It just isn't natural."

"Make no mistake." Yankel looked up from is plate for a moment. "When I finish this borsht, will I give a yell!"

☺ ☺ ☺ ☺ ☺ ☺ ☺ ☺

The Storekeeper

An elderly Jewish storekeeper is struck by a speeding taxi-cab. Surviving the impact, he is brought to Mount Sinai Medical Center. A nurse gently tucks him into bed and asks, "Mr. Levy, are you comfortable?"

He nods. "I make a nice living."

☺ ☺ ☺ ☺ ☺ ☺ ☺ ☺

Making You Smart

A customer of Harvey's Kosher Fish store marveled at Harvey's fast wit and the fact that he had an answer to everything under the sun.

"Tell me, Harvey, just what is it that makes you so smart?"

Harvey responded: "It's eating herring heads. If you eat enough of them, you'll be a veritable genius."

"Do you have them in stock?"

"Yes, I do, and they are a buck a piece."

The customer took three. A week later he came back and complained that he hadn't gotten any smarter.

"You didn't eat enough of them," said Harvey.

This time the customer spent twenty dollars on twenty fish. Two weeks passed and he was angrier than ever. "Hey, Harvey," he shouted, "you're gypping me. You sell me a whole herring for fifty cents. Why should I pay a buck for a herring head?"

"You see," said Harvey, "how much smarter you are already?"

☺ ☺ ☺ ☺ ☺ ☺ ☺ ☺

Two Martians

Two Martians who had arrived on different flying saucers ran into each other on Madison Avenue.

The first asked, "So, tell me, what's your name?"

"Eight-four-three-nine-one."

The first one smiled, and with his three eyes, said: "That's funny, you don't look Jewish."

☺ ☺ ☺ ☺ ☺ ☺ ☺ ☺

Jewish Fundraising

As Mendel was walking down Fifth Avenue, he encountered a Jewish fundraiser.

"Please, can you give me ten dollars?" asks the fundraiser.

"What do you need it for?" asks Mendel.

"For a cup of coffee," replies the fundraiser.

"But a cup of coffee is only two dollars," says Mendel.

"I know," says the fundraiser, "but I'm a big tipper."

☺ ☺ ☺ ☺ ☺ ☺ ☺ ☺

Weizmann's Reply

In the years before the Balfour Declaration, a member of the House of Lords asked Chaim Weizmann, "Why do you Jews insist on Palestine when there are so many undeveloped countries for your consideration?"

Weizmann replied: "That is like my asking you why you drove thirty miles to visit your mother last Sunday when there are so many old ladies living on your street."

☺ ☺ ☺ ☺ ☺ ☺ ☺ ☺

Drycleaning

Walking through New York's Chinatown, a Canadian tourist was enjoying the artistry of all of the Chinese restaurants, shops, and signs, when he turned a corner and saw a building with the sign Moishe Plotnik's Laundry.

"Moishe Plotnik?" he wondered. "How does that belong in Chinatown?"

He walked into the shop and saw a fairly standard-looking drycleaner, although he could see that the owners were clearly aware of the uniqueness of the store name as there were baseball caps, T-shirts, and sweatshirts all with the logo Moishe Plotnik's Chinese Laundry.

The tourist selected a coffee cup as a conversation piece to take back to his office. Behind the counter was a smiling Chinese man who thanked him for his purchase. The tourist then asked, "Can you explain to me how this place got a name like Moishe Plotnik's Laundry?"

The man answered, "Evleebody ask me that. It name of owner."

Looking around, the tourist asked, "Is the owner here?
"It me," replies the man.

"Really? You're Chinese. How did you get a name like Moishe Plotnik?"

"Is simple," said the old man. "Many many year ago I come to this country. I standing in line at Documentation Center of Immigration. Man in front of me was Jewish man from Poland. Lady at counter look at him and say, 'What your name?'

"He say Moishe Plotnik.
"Then she look at me and say, 'What your name?'
"I say Sam Ting."

☺ ☺ ☺ ☺ ☺ ☺ ☺ ☺

Garden of Eden
In one respect, life in the Garden of Eden must have been exceptionally difficult for Adam and Eve. Poor souls, they had no one to gossip about.

☺ ☺ ☺ ☺ ☺ ☺ ☺ ☺

Friends
Four Jewish friends met religiously once a week for lunch and an afternoon of playing cards. On one occasion, one of them blurted out a long-held secret to the others, saying: "I have a confession to make, something I have to get off my chest. I'm a kleptomaniac. But please don't worry. You are the best friends in the whole world. I would never take anything that belongs to any of you."

Hearing her confession, a second member of the group spoke up: "I, too, have something to confess. I'm a nymphomaniac, but please don't let this upset you. You are my dearest friends. I have never had an affair with your husbands, and I never will."

A third member of the group felt impelled to make her own confession. "I'm a lesbian, but out of respect for each of you and for our friendship, I will never attempt to involve any of you sexually."

At this, the fourth friend spoke up: "I, too, have a secret to confess. I'm a gossip, so please excuse me. I have an urgent call to make."

☺ ☺ ☺ ☺ ☺ ☺ ☺ ☺

Woman in Labor

A worried Jew, something of an ignoramus, met a friend who immediately recognized that something was troubling him. In response to his query, he replied, "My wife has been in labor for two weeks and is in great distress." His friend said, "I know a remedy for her. We can do it for her immediately. All we need are ten pious men to gather at her bedside and recite the Book of Psalms."

The grateful husband quickly rounded up a group of ten men and brought them to his wife's room, where they began to recite Psalms. A few minutes later the midwife shooed them out of the room. Within moments she emerged, shouting to the husband, "Good news! Your wife has given birth to a son."

The husband ran to the bedroom but was stopped at the door by the midwife, "You cannot enter just now. She's in the middle of delivering a second one." The same thing happened a third time. Noticing that the ten men were still reciting Psalms aloud, he shouted to them, "Stop reciting immediately!"

☺ ☺ ☺ ☺ ☺ ☺ ☺ ☺

The Real Gefilte Fish

I have often been upset by people who seem to think that gefilte fish is some kind of mixture you make in the kitchen rather than one of the Lord's creatures. This has led me to try to explain exactly what gefilte fish is. So here goes:

Each year, as soon as the ice on the Great Gefilte Lakes (located in upstate New York, somewhere in the Catskill Mountains) is frum (observant), fishermen set out to catch gefilte fish. Now, unlike your normal fish, gefilte fish cannot be caught with a rod and a reel or standard bait. The art of catching gefilte fish has been handed down for hundreds, maybe thousands of generations. For all I know, Moses used to go gefilte fishing. I'm sure that the Great Rambam (Maimonides), when he wasn't playing doctor, spent his leisure time gefilte fishing.

Enough already, you say, so how is it done? Well, you go to the edge of the lake with some matzah. Now this is very important. It has to be Manischewitz matzah or the fish will not be attracted to it. You stand at the edge of the lake and whistle and say, "Here, boy!" "Here, boy!" The fish just can't resist the smell of the matzah. They come together to the edge of the lake, where they jump into the jars and are bottled on the spot.

Last year, a well-meaning gentleman tried to correct me: "Shouldn't they be saying 'Here, boychik' and not 'Here, boy?'" I didn't have the heart to tell him that *boychik* is a Yiddish word and gefilte fish don't understand Yiddish—only Hebrew and, surprisingly, English! (There is an ongoing debate as to whether to use the Hebrew or English in the U.S.)

A Potpourri of Jewish Humor

In a shocking break with tradition, the English is accepted by almost all gefilte fishermen. The Congress of OU Rabbis (who have to be present at the lakes when the fish are bottled) uniformly accept "Here, boy!" although some holdouts still insist on using the Hebrew and consider the use of "Here, boy" as Reform and not acceptable.

You must remember that there are two kinds of gefilte fish. The strong and the weak. The weak are your standard fish, which are in a loose "broth." (Is it actually the lake water?) Now the strong ones are really special. They seem to be in a "jell." These fish don't come from the Great Gefilte Lakes. They are actually imported from the Middle East, where they are caught in the Dead Sea. They have to be strong enough to be able to swim through that jell.

The timing of the catch is very important. The fish cannot be caught before Purim is over or they are considered chametz (leaven). (Besides, the fish know when Passover is coming, and will not respond to the matzah bait before the proper time).

I am still a little bothered by which end of the gefilte fish is the head and which the tail (not to mention that I am not sure where their eyes are). This is a small price to pay for the luxury of eating this delicacy. Have you ever tried the baby gefilte fish? Oy, they are so cute that I feel a little guilty eating them!

I hope that the matzah doesn't affect you like Pepto-Bismol or, worse yet, prunes. For the Pepto crowd there is some relief: there is a new product available in the stores this year, called Metamatzil. You can find it easily.

Just look for the logo on the box: "LET MY PEOPLE GO"
Wishing you all a Happy Passover!

☺ ☺ ☺ ☺ ☺ ☺ ☺ ☺

Small Town Jew
A Jew from a little town made his first visit to the big city. For the first time in his entire life, he entered a restaurant and asked to be served a meal. The waiter gave him a menu and quickly realized that he was dealing with a naive country yokel. He brought him a plate of stale, reheated leftovers. After finishing his meal, the customer left the restaurant and soon developed a horrible stomachache. He entered an alley where he threw up his entire meal.

A policeman spotted him and fined him ten rubles for dirtying city property.

The Jew became confused. "Officer," he said, "I don't at all understand this. It cost me one ruble to buy a meal. Why should it cost me ten rubles to throw it up?"

☺ ☺ ☺ ☺ ☺ ☺ ☺ ☺

The Laws of Passover
An advanced class was studying Talmud with a melamed (teacher) who was less than advanced. Their topic was a section dealing with the Passover laws. Among the foods considered acceptable for the Passover seder meal, the Talmud mentions one called *tamchah* (a type of bitter herb).

One of the students asked, "What is the meaning of *tamchah*?" The melamed, not very sure himself how to translate the word, immediately instructed him to look it up in Rashi's (French Bible commentator) commentary.

The child did as he was asked. He saw that Rashi had written, "This will be explained later in the chapter."

He turned the pages and saw that the Talmud quotes the cryptic words of a sage who explains that *tamcha* is the same as *temachta*. Again, the student questioned the melamed, "Teacher, what is *temachta*?"

The teacher responded: "Did I not tell you to read what Rashi says?"

The student replied, "I did look at the Rashi comment, and he says, *temachta* is the same as *marubiya*." [Note: Rashi frequently uses French to explain Talmudic words.]

The student, now more puzzled than before, asked again, "But what is *marubiya*?"

The malamed, exasperated by the child's questions and frustrated by his own ignorance, blurted out, "Go ask a Frenchman!"

☺ ☺ ☺ ☺ ☺ ☺ ☺ ☺

The Biggest Loser

Harry Kline, who took the New York Bar State exam twenty-two times finally passed in 1958. He then practiced law for eighteen years without acquiring a single client. In sheer desperation, Mr. Kline filed suit for divorce against his own wife so he would have at least one case before he retired. He lost the case!

☺ ☺ ☺ ☺ ☺ ☺ ☺ ☺

The Funeral

Sometime after Beryl died, his widow Shoshana was finally able to speak about what a beautiful man her late husband had been.

"Beryl thought of everything," she told them. "Just before he died, he called me to his bedside and handed me three envelopes, telling me that in them were his three last wishes. When he died," she said, "he said that it would be time to open the envelopes and follow the instructions."

"What was in the envelopes?" her friends asked.

"Well, in the first one there was $3,000 in cash with a note that said to buy a nice all-wooden casket. So I bought a beautiful oak one to fulfill his wishes.

"The second envelop contained $7,000 in cash, with a note telling me to make him a nice funeral."

"What was in the third envelope?" the friends asked.

She replied: "The third envelope contained $50,000 in cash with a note: 'Please use this to buy the nicest stone.'"

Holding her hand in the air, Shoshana said: "So, do you like my stone?" showing off her fifteen-carat diamond ring.

☺ ☺ ☺ ☺ ☺ ☺ ☺ ☺

The Empty Seat

Chayyim Yankel was enjoying himself at the New York Giants game until he noticed an empty seat down in front.

He went down and asked the fellow next to it if he knew whose seat it was. The guy said, "Yes, that's my wife's seat. We have never missed a game, but now my wife is dead." Chayim offered his sympathies and said it was really a shame that he couldn't find some other relative to give the ticket to so that they could enjoy the game together.

"Oh, no," the guy said. They're all at the funeral."

☺ ☺ ☺ ☺ ☺ ☺ ☺ ☺

Japanese Bar Mitzvah
Mendel was telling his friend Muttel a joke: "Shapiro and Rosenzweig were talking one day . . ."

Right away, his friend Muttel interrupts him. "Always with the Jewish jokes. Come one, give it a rest. Why do they always have to be about Jews? Don't you know any jokes that aren't about Jews?"

So Mendel starts again. "Okay, Hideki and Hashimoto were talking one day at their niece's bat mitzvah . . ."

☺ ☺ ☺ ☺ ☺ ☺ ☺ ☺

The Most Common Lines from Bar Mitzvah Speeches
1. The first candle will be lit by—
2. If only my Aunt Minnie could be here—
3. Today, I am an Israeli bond.
4. It's a great thrill to finally be bar-mitzvahed, because now I can finally drop out of Hebrew school and be in the school play.

5. I can hardly wait to get home and see what's in these envelopes so many of you gave me.

☺ ☺ ☺ ☺ ☺ ☺ ☺ ☺

The Greatest Lyrics of Chasidic Pop Tunes
YA BA BA BA BA BA BA BA BA BA BA BA BA
Chorus: LA LA LA LA LA LA LA LA LA LA
Second verse: OY YOY YOY OY YOY YOY OY YOY YOY
Chorus: LA LA LA LA LA LA LA LA LA LA LA LA
Third Verse: BIM BAM BIM BAM BIM BAM BIM BAM
Chorus: LA LA LA LA LA LA LA LA

☺ ☺ ☺ ☺ ☺ ☺ ☺ ☺

Happiest Wedding Announcement
When their fifty-year-old daughter Shulamit finally received a marriage proposal, her joyous parents, Mr. and Mrs. Pinchas Leviner, sent out the following wedding announcement:

Mr. And Mrs. Pinchas Leviner are greatly relieved to announce the long-awaited marriage of their single daughter, Shulamit, to somebody.

☺ ☺ ☺ ☺ ☺ ☺ ☺ ☺

Who Will Lead the Prayer Service?
A poor Jew had completed the required time of mourning for his deceased wife. To mark the occasion, he wished to lead the prayer service at the synagogue. As he walked to the lectern, a rich man elbowed past him and said, "I

have priority over you. I am still within the first thirty days of mourning. At this, a third person, also wealthy, stepped forward and announced, "My priority is higher than both of yours. Today, I am observing the anniversary of the death of my father."

A fourth man, even more wealthy, pushed his way to the lectern and proclaimed, "None of your have priority over me. I am still in the midst of the first seven days of mourning."

He was about to lead the service when a pale person, robed in white, entered the prayer chapel and called out in a hollow voice, "I shall lead the service. I am the deceased."

☺   ☺   ☺   ☺   ☺   ☺   ☺   ☺

An International Purim

King Ahasuerus was Finnish with his disobedient wife Vashti. "You Congo now!" he ordered. After she had Ghana way, the king's messengers went Roman the land to find a new queen. And India end, the beautiful Esther won the crown.

Meanwhile, Mordecai sat outside the palace, where the Child Haman would Czech up on him daily.

"I Haiti you because you refuse to bow down to me," Haman scolded Mordecai. "USA very stubborn man. Yu Jews are such Bahamas! If you keep his up, Denmark my words: I will have all your people killed. Just Kuwait and see, you Turkey."

Mordecai went into mourning and tore his clothes—a custom known as Korea. He urged Esther to plead with the king. The Jews fasted for three days and grew very Hungary. Esther approached the king and asked, "Kenya Belize come to a banquet I've prepared for you and Haman?"

At the feast she invited her guests to a second banquet to eat Samoa.

The king asked, "Esther, why Jamaica big meal like this? Just tell me what you want. Unto half my United Kingdom will I give you." Esther replied, "Spain full for me to say this, but Haman is Russian to kill my people."

Haman's loud Wales could be heard as he carried Honduran this scene. "Oman!" Haman cried bitterly. "Iraq my brains in an effort to destroy the Jews. But that sneaky Mordecai—Egypt me!"

Haman and his ten sons were hanged and went immediately to the Netherlands. And to Sweden the deal, the Jews were allowed to Polish off the rest of their foes as well. "You lost your enemies and Uganda friend," the king smiled.

And that is why the Purim story Israeli a miracle. God decided to China light on His chosen people.

So now, let's celebrate. Forget all your Syria's business and just be happy. Serb up some wine and Taiwan on! Happy Purim!

☺   ☺   ☺   ☺   ☺   ☺   ☺   ☺

Wait for the Meat
During one severe winter in Russia, the Jews are very hungry. The town council announces that meat will be arriving shortly, so everyone gets on line to be the first to get

the meat. After two hours of waiting in the snow and the cold, the council announces that there will be much less meat coming than first expected and tells all the Jews to go home.

Another hour passes, and again the town council announces that there will be less food arriving than expected, and that all non-communists should now go home. All the non-communists leave the line.

Another hour passes, and the town council announces that there will be no food arriving, and everybody should go home.

As one man trudges through the snow, he turns to his friend and says, "You see, the Jews always get to go home first!"

☺ ☺ ☺ ☺ ☺ ☺ ☺ ☺

Weird Dream

Feivel was talking to his psychiatrist. "I had a strange dream recently," he says. "I saw my mother, but then I noticed that she had your face. I found this so worrying that I immediately woke up and couldn't get back to sleep. I just stayed there thinking about it until 7 a.m. I got up, made myself toast and coffee, and came straight here. Can you please help me explain the meaning of my dream?"

The psychiatrist kept silent for some time then said, "One slice of toast and coffee. Do you call that a breakfast?"

☺ ☺ ☺ ☺ ☺ ☺ ☺ ☺

The Beggars

Two beggars are sitting on the pavement in Ireland. One is holding a large cross and the other a Star of David. Both are holding hats to collect contributions. As people walk by, they lift their noses at the guy holding the Star of David, but drop money in the other guy's hat. Soon one hat is nearly full while the other is empty.

The priest watches and then approaches the men. He turns to the guy with the Star of David and says, "Don't you realize this is a Christian country? You'll never get any contributions in this country holding a Star of David."

The guy holding the Star of David then turns to the guy holding the cross and says, "Hymie, look who's trying to teach us marketing."

☺ ☺ ☺ ☺ ☺ ☺ ☺ ☺

The Prize

Marie was nearing sixty-five and was in her final year of teaching. She was a devout Christian who missed teaching from the Bible. She then decided that she was going to disregard the new school regulations and teach religion. She told her class that she would hold a contest, and would give fifty bucks to the student who could tell her the greatest man who ever lived.

Immediately Moishe began to wave his hand, but Marie ignored him in favor of those in her Sunday School class. As she went around the room, Marie was disappointed with the answers she got. Jane, her best scholar, picked Noah, because he saved all of the animals. Others said, "I think the greatest man who ever lived was Alexander the

Great, because he conquered the entire world." Another said: "I think it was Thomas Edison, because he invented the light bulb."

Finally, Marie called on Moishe, who still had his hand in the air.

"I think the greatest man who ever lived was Jesus," said Moishe. Marie was shocked but still gave him the fifty dollars' reward. As she did so, she said, "Well, Moishe, I'm very surprised that you should be the only one with the right answer."

"Well, to tell you the truth," Moshe replied as he pocketed the money, "I think it was Moses, but business is business."

☺ ☺ ☺ ☺ ☺ ☺ ☺ ☺

Jewish Grandmother

A little Jewish grandmother gets on the crowded bus and discovers that she doesn't have the correct change for the fare. The driver tries to be firm with her, but she places her hand delicately over her chest and murmurs, "If you knew what I had, you'd be nicer to me."

He caves in and lets her ride free.

She tries to push her way down the crowded aisle, but people won't move over for her. She finally places her hand delicately over her chest and murmurs, "If you knew what I had, you'd be nicer to me." The crowd parts like the Red Sea and lets her down the aisle. She gets to the back of the bus where there are no seats and looks significantly at several people, none of whom take the hint to get up to offer her their seat.

Once again she places her hand delicately over her chest and murmurs, "If you knew what I had, you'd be nicer to me."

Several people jump up and insist that she sit down and ride in comfort.

A woman who had been watching all this leaned over and said to her, "I know this is none of my business, but just what is it that you've got anyway?"

The little grandmother smiled and said, "Chutzpah" (nerve).

☺ ☺ ☺ ☺ ☺ ☺ ☺ ☺

Jewish Dog
Morty visits the vet and says, "My dog has a problem."

The vet replies: "So what's your dog's problem?"
"First you should know that he's a Jewish dog. His name is Irving and he can talk," says Morty.

"He can talk?" the doubtful doctor asks.

"Watch this!" Morty points to the dog and commands: "Irving, fetch!"

Irving the dog begins to walk toward the door, and then turns around and demands, "So why are you talking to me like that? You order me around like I'm nothing. And you only call me when you want something. And then you make me sleep on the floor with my arthritis. You give me this awful food and you tell me it's a special diet. It tastes horrible. You should eat it yourself. And do you ever take me for a decent walk. No, it's out of the house, a short walk, and back in again."

The doctor is amazed. "This is remarkable. What could be the problem?"

Morty answers, "Obviously he has a hearing problem. I said 'fetch,' not 'kvetch'" (complain).

☺ ☺ ☺ ☺ ☺ ☺ ☺ ☺

The New Hearing Aid

An elderly Jewish fellow had serious hearing problems for a number of years. He went to a specialist who was able to have him fitted for a set of hearing aids that allowed him to hear one hundred percent. A month later he went back to the doctor, who said: "Your hearing is perfect. Your family must be really pleased that you can hear again."

The fellow replied: "Oh, I haven't told my family yet. I just sit around and listen to the conversations. I've changed my will three times!"

☺ ☺ ☺ ☺ ☺ ☺ ☺ ☺

The Insider Trader

An old Jewish man lived alone in the country. He wanted to dig his potato garden, but it was very hard work since the ground was so hard. His only son, Saul, who used to help him, was in prison for insider trading and stock fraud.

The old man wrote a letter to his son and described his predicament.

Dear Solly,
I am feeling pretty bad because it looks like I won't

be able to plant my potato garden this year. I'm just getting too old to be digging up a garden plot. If you were here, all my troubles would be over. I know you would dig the plot for me.

Love,
Papa

A few days later the old man received a letter from his son.

Dear Papa,
For heaven's sake, dad, don't dig up that garden. That's where I buried the money and stocks.

Love,
Solly

At four in the morning the next day, a team of FBI agents and local police arrived at the old man's house and dug up the entire garden area without finding any money or stocks. They apologized to the old man and left.

That very same day the old man received another letter from his son.

Dear Papa,
Go ahead and plant the potatoes now. That's the best I could do under the circumstances.

Love,
Your son,
Solly

A Few Laughs

Q. Why did Adam and Eve have a perfect marriage?

A. He didn't have to hear about all the men she could have married, and she didn't have to hear about the way his mother cooked.

Q. How do Jewish wives get their kids ready for supper?

A. They put them in the car.

Q. What is the technical term for a divorced woman?

A. Plaintiff.

Q. If Tarzan and Jane were Jewish, what would Cheetah be?

A. A fur coat.

☺ ☺ ☺ ☺ ☺ ☺ ☺ ☺

Nisht in Shabbos Gereht

Note: Nisht in Shabbos Gereht is a statement that religious Jews use on the Sabbath when they are about to say something inappropriate for Sabbath discussion.

Two guys are sitting in synagogue on Shabbat morning when the first guy says to the second guy, rather quietly and secretively, "Nisht in Shabbos Gereht, but I've put my car up for sale." The second guy responds, just as quietly and just as secretively: Nisht in Shabbos Gereht, but what kind of car is it?"

First guy: "Nisht in Shabbos Gereht, but it's a Cadillac, late model, low mileage, and is in creampuff condition.

Second Guy: "Nisht in Shabbos Gereht, but how much are you asking for it?"

First Guy: "Nisht in Shabbos Gereht, but I'm asking $15,000."

Second Guy: "Nisht in Shabbos Gereht, but let me think about it."

They meet again in the after at Mincha prayer services, when the second guy corners the first guy says quietly, "Nisht in Shabbos Gereht, but I'll offer you 12 for it."

The first guy responds. "Nisht in Shabbos Gereht, but I sold it already."

☺ ☺ ☺ ☺ ☺ ☺ ☺ ☺

Chasidim

The story is told of two men visiting New York City for the first time who come across two Jews wearing long black coats, wide-brimmed hats with long beards and earlocks. One man turns to the other and says, "What's that?"

The second man replies, "Chasidim."

The first man responds, "I see them, too, but what are they?"

☺ ☺ ☺ ☺ ☺ ☺ ☺ ☺

Bubbe's Computer

Tech Support: "What kind of computer do you have?"

Bubbe: "A white one. I can't get my diskette out."

Tech support: "Have you tried pushing the button?"

Bubbe: "Yes, sure, it's really stuck."

Tech support: "That doesn't sound good. I'll make a note."

Bubbe: "No, wait a minute, I hadn't inserted it yet. It's still on my desk."

Tech Support: "Click on the My Computer icon to the left of the screen."

Bubbe: "Your left or my left?"

Tech Support: "Okay, let's press the Control and Escape keys at the same time. That brings up a task list in the middle of the screen. Now type the letter *p* to bring up the Program Manager."

Bubbe: "I don't have a *p*."

Tech support: "On your keyboard."

Bubbe: "What do you mean?"

Tech support: "*P*, on your keyboard."

Bubbe: "I'm not going to do that!"

☺ ☺ ☺ ☺ ☺ ☺ ☺ ☺